MOVING
IN THE POWER
OF GOD

BRENT DOUGLAS

Brent Douglas
www.brentdouglas.co.nz
© 2015 by Brent Douglas.
First published 2015.

All rights reserved. No part of this book may be reproduced or transmitted in any form or by any means for commercial gain without written permission from the author. The use of short quotations or occasional page copying for personal or group study is permitted and encouraged.

Unless otherwise indicated, Scripture quotations are from the NEW AMERICAN STANDARD BIBLE © 1960, 1962, 1963, 1968, 1971, 1972, 1075, 1977, 1995 The Lockman Foundation.

ISBN 978-0-473-33478-9 (paperback)
ISBN 978-0-473-33479-6 (ebook)

Cover design by Nathan Chambers, The Art Co.
Typeset by BookPrint Ltd. www.bookprint.co.nz

CONTENTS

Foreword v

Preface ix

Foundational Concepts for Moving in the Power of God 13

Three Elements of a Move of God 33

Sustaining a Move of the Spirit in the Local Church 57

Using the Five Physical Senses 123

God is Moving, Now What? 147

FOREWORD

My message and my preaching were not with wise and persuasive words, but with a demonstration of the Spirit's power, so that your faith might not rest on human wisdom, but on God's power. (1 Corinthians 2:4-5)

In 1993, a unique outpouring of the Holy Spirit began flooding into churches in New Zealand, as was the case in many other parts of the world. All of a sudden we went from being pastors and Christian leaders who were hungering for a fresh move of God, to men and women needing to learn how to effectively flow with this "river of joy and power" and be proper stewards of the most amazing things we'd ever witnessed in all our years of service in the Kingdom.

It was during those early years of this outpouring that it became clear to my colleagues and I that

God was raising up a man among us who would enable and equip us in these happy and precious things – and now that man, Pastor Brent Douglas, has committed two decades of "demonstration and power" to the pages of this book.

For over twenty years, Brent has powerfully stewarded the move of the Holy Spirit in New Zealand, and beyond. I have seen him teach and demonstrate how to move in the prophetical and power gifts of the Holy Spirit in workshops, pastors' seminars, ministry training schools, youth conferences and local church ministry – to thousands.

It's easy to vividly recall his visits to the Fiji Islands – and laugh out loud as much as simply stand in awe! For four years my wife and I lived in the midst of the Fijian revival with a charge to facilitate the training of men and women who would become pastors, church planters and missionaries throughout the South Pacific, to unreached people groups, and in villages and cities in practically every continent on earth. It was never in question as to whom I would ask to come and equip these "sold out" young people to be men and women of the Spirit. With characteristic boldness and good humour, Brent soon had our students moving in words of knowledge, discerning and dealing with demonic strongholds, imparting the anointing with manifestations of power and prophesying boldly.

Of course any learning-curve is accompanied with harmless mistakes – often hilarious and sometimes potentially embarrassing. However, Brent's obvious love for these eager learners dissolved any tension and quickly turned every situation into laughter-filled teaching moments. There are now hundreds of men and women around the world – some in the most primitive of settings – who are carrying revival with the confidence to bring encounters with God wherever they go.

It is easy to feel intimidated by the call to be able ministers of the Spirit – that is probably the reason why we retreat to the safety of the pulpit rather than roll up our sleeves and flow with the Spirit as Jesus and the early apostles did so naturally. But expect something special to happen as you read this book. You are going to find faith and courage will be imparted through its pages, just as faith and courage would rise when Pastor Brent was equipping in a "live" workshop or pastor's training session. As much as Brent equipped and enabled us, he also restored us to faith and function whenever the weariness and buffeting of ministry life was taking its toll. Happily, I can now have those "wells of refreshing" on my desk alongside my Bible and laptop.

In my life, and that of hundreds I know, there has been no better practitioner of the Apostle Paul's mandate to demonstrate the Spirit's power, and to equip the saints for the work of the ministry. That will be obvious to you in what you are about to read.

— *David Collins*

Pastor, church planter, teacher, and missionary
Auckland, New Zealand

PREFACE

There is one thing that I have come to understand: people, particularly Christians, once they become aware of the potential of moving in and experiencing the power of God, deeply desire to personally experience this dimension of supernatural experience. I personally had a powerful experience of the power of God in the 1970s when I received the Baptism of the Holy Spirit. For 1½ hours the power of God dramatically touched me to such a level I could never be satisfied with anything less for the remainder of my Christian experience. Not only that, but I have continued to see during 30 years of Christian ministry, thousands of lives changed through experiencing the supernatural power of the Spirit.

Issues that have been long standing controls and burdens have been frequently healed through a moment's encounter with the Holy Spirit. Frequently, when the power of God is moving, issues are flushed to the surface in people's lives, even demonic controls, and the issues are overcome, often permanently.

"So it will be in that day, that his burden will be removed from your shoulders and his yoke from your neck, and the yoke will be broken because of fatness." (Isaiah 10:27) Another way of putting this is: *"…and the yoke shall be destroyed because of the anointing."* (Isaiah 10:27 KJV)

The manifest anointing of the Holy Spirit will destroy yokes of bondage in people's lives. This was fundamental to Jesus' ministry and He set the dimensions clearly: *"The Spirit of the Lord is upon Me, because He anointed Me to preach the gospel to the poor. He has sent Me to proclaim release to the captives, And recovery of sight to the blind, to set free those who are oppressed…"* (Luke 4:18)

These results are all because *"The Spirit of the Lord is upon Me…"* That is the manifest power of God.

My intention here is not to present a case for the power of God moving in the church and Christians' lives today. That is taken for granted. The intent here is to equip leaders, pastors and others who desire to lead people into power encounters of the

Holy Spirit in the ways this can be achieved on a consistent basis. It is my belief that there is no reason why we cannot regularly experience mighty encounters with the power of God.

New Zealand is like most nations; full of churches doing a great job but obviously because of their size and the community they minister in, lacking the resources of music and gifting to bring a consistent level of effective praise and worship, and a positive encouraging atmosphere. And yet they deeply yearn for a move of the Spirit. They will look to other churches and other countries for places where the Spirit of God is moving and seek this out without knowing how they can bring this power dimension to their own church.

I had to work out the principles of moving in the power of God to bring that manifest anointing in any environment whether or not I was given a great atmosphere to minister out from. What if the music was awful? What if the congregation were not fully connected and participating in what was happening? Did this mean I couldn't move in the power of God and bring the congregation into a renewal of Holy Spirit encounter? So many travelling ministries are dependent on the atmosphere created prior to their getting up to minister. If they are not handed a great atmosphere following the praise and worship then they are not able to move in the power of God. But so many of the churches I ministered in could not present that level of free and anointed atmosphere.

I had to discover a way that the congregation could receive supernatural encounters with the power of God whether a great atmosphere was handed to me or not. Just because the praise and worship was not good, that surely did not mean the power of God couldn't move in significant ways. Why should I be dependent on what was handed to me at the end of the praise and worship? Therefore, what were the principles of moving in the Spirit that could enhance the possibility of the Spirit of God moving powerfully?

I want to share the principles that I have learnt that have enabled me to see the power of God move in many and varied environments, churches and atmospheres. The secrets here are the result of 30 years of consistently seeing churches in New Zealand and overseas come into their own revival and release of Holy Spirit freedom.

CHAPTER 1:
FOUNDATIONAL CONCEPTS FOR MOVING IN THE POWER OF GOD

There are some foundations that we need to adopt in order to experience the power of God consistently and regularly.

God Is Moving All the Time, He Has Never Stopped Moving

It is a fatal error to think that God is not moving. God is and has been moving all the time. He wants to touch His people. He wants His church fully experiencing the power of God. He desires to see His church set free. Yet so often one attends prayer meetings with Christians praying and asking God to move in the service that is about to occur. But why would they pray such a prayer? Has God stopped moving and does He somehow need to be stirred to move, to release His power, to once again encounter the people of God? This is so demeaning toward God. And so congregations are ever hopeful that someday, somehow, God might awaken from His sleep and choose to touch His church. This is so against the fundamental understanding of a loving Heavenly Father who celebrates His children, rejoicing over them with singing.

Like any father who wants to celebrate life with his children, God wants to allow His children to experience His best. And His best is always connected to His Spirit bringing heaven to earth. What a mean spirited God who would leave His people having to cry out for Him to move and touch His people. Such thinking is based upon an Old Testament view of God where faith people are ever seeking the approval of God and not upon a grace-filled God who loves us.

So what is the problem? The answer is simple and clear: the problem is not that God is not moving by His Spirit. The problem is not that God is somehow withholding from us. No! He is already moving and wanting to touch His people. The problem is that we are not moving in power and faith. We are not accessing the resources of heaven. We are not creating a way in which God is able to encounter His people. Nor are we building an environment of faith and expectancy that creates a *pregnant* atmosphere. God has already given the responsibility of leading His church to His leadership. But if the leadership fail in their responsibility to access the power of God and to release that power to the people of God, then of course we are left wondering why God is not moving. The principle of seeing the power of God moving requires the initiative to come from us. Jesus demonstrated this time and again in His own ministry.

Talking to the woman at the well He brilliantly manoeuvred the conversation in order to bring to the woman what clearly was a word of knowledge as expressed in 1 Corinthians 14 to the woman. He delivered the supernatural knowledge by eventually informing her that indeed the man she was living with was not her husband and in fact she had had five husbands. The effect was that she went back to her village, reported what had occurred, and the city came out to see who had spoken such a thing. This precipitated a significant revival. But the issue is that Jesus had to take the initiative for the revival to be unlocked. The disciples soon learnt this lesson. The cripple waiting at the temple gate in Acts 3 would have remained a cripple for the rest of his life if Peter and John had chosen this time to give him some money. Instead they decided to step out in faith and pray for him to be healed. The initiative had to come from Peter and John.

And so it is that God is waiting for us to take the initiative, move in the power of God and bring the people of God into the experiences of the Holy Spirit that are so readily available. We must not use the excuse that we couldn't move in the power of God because the praise and worship didn't quite make it. We cannot use the excuse that we couldn't move in the power of God because the atmosphere wasn't somehow right.

No, the initiative must come from the leadership. It is understood that it is harder than preaching a message. It is easy to deliver a sermon rather than step out from the podium and declare the fact that God is about to move. Faith is required to seek a move of the Spirit amongst a group of believers. We have to face the fear of failure, of making a fool of ourselves, of the fact that maybe nothing will happen. But we must start somewhere, somehow. Learn from our mistakes but eventually learn how to access heaven and impact earth in the arena where God has led us to minister.

Of course we cannot deliver to the congregation what the leader has not personally experienced. It goes without saying that all Christian leaders should be baptised in the Holy Spirit; that their Baptism of the Spirit should be as Jesus described:

…but you will receive power when the Holy Spirit has come upon you; and you shall be My witnesses both in Jerusalem, and in all Judea and Samaria, and even to the remotest part of the earth. (Acts 1:8)

Jesus describes here that it is a receiving of power; supernatural power. Power is something that is always a discernible, clearly felt dimension. Put your finger in a live power socket and you will experience power! It is the same with the power of God, but the power is far greater than a natural power socket. It is supernatural power and therefore will have a supernatural impact when experienced. The example throughout the book of Acts is that when people received the Baptism of the Spirit it was often experienced with accompanying dramatic supernatural encounters. So many believers have been robbed of this by settling for a Baptism of the Spirit that was anything other than a powerful encounter of the spirit. It is contingent on all believers to not settle for something that clearly is not the intention of Jesus.

The foundation for the early church was a people who had encountered the power of God in a dramatic manner. We must not settle for less! Too often we will change our belief systems to incorporate our failure to enter into all that God has for us. We don't have a power encounter with the Holy Spirit? Then we change the doctrine and adjust the belief system so that *our* failure to receive is excused. This must stop. If we are not receiving a biblical experience then we need to set our hearts toward having the experience and do whatever is necessary to *enter in*. I myself did not receive the Baptism of the Spirit when first prayed for, but I was determined to break through. The second time I was prayed for I did receive *a touch*, but I still was not released into the full experience of the Baptism of the Spirit. But I kept praying, kept believing. I was determined! On the third occasion I had my breakthrough, as previously described. That encounter has continued for 30 years in various levels of intensity. I have constantly taken opportunities to receive prayer and impartation for personal empowerment and renewal. The Bible states in Ephesians 5:18: *"And do not get drunk with wine, for that is dissipation, but be filled with the Spirit…"*

One of the meanings of *"be filled"* in Greek is *to cram up*. I want to be *crammed up* with the power of God. Why would we be satisfied with anything less? What religious mind-sets would allow us to be satisfied with less than being crammed up with the power of God?

I love the example of Paul in Acts 13:52: *"And the disciples were continually filled with joy and with the Holy Spirit."* They were continually crammed up with joy and with the Holy Spirit. That doesn't sound like a Christian walk devoid of power encounters of the Holy Spirit.

Over many years I have noticed a pattern concerning people whom God is using in remarkable ways. I will ask them, "What was the encounter you had with God, that you would point to, which released you into the dimensions of power that you currently move in?" In every instance, if they trust me, they will share deep and personal, mighty Holy Spirit encounters that became the launching pad for their ministry. They will rarely preach and share about these experiences for fear of criticism and rejection, but they know that these were their initiation into the impacting ministry they now move in.

But does God love them more than you and me? Are they somehow special and we are not? God is not prejudiced against one person versus another, but often there was a hunger that drew them into seeking a personal breakthrough.

I used to pray on Saturday nights in a park where I would speak in tongues until such a time that the Holy Spirit would show me what He wanted to do in the Sunday morning service. One particular night I felt the Lord say to me, "I want you to release joy in the congregation tomorrow morning." I knew this meant more than just *being happy*. This was about people being released in laughter. I had no idea how to release joy in a congregation, on top of which, I was not free in the joy of the Lord. I replied, "Lord how can I release something I don't have? If you want me to release joy in the morning then I need to first experience supernatural joy so that I can give something I already have."

I continued in prayer and walking around the park when suddenly I came to a spot and the joy of the Lord *hit* me. I began to laugh. I remained there for a time laughing, then continued to walk around the park, praying and marvelling at the experience, until I came back to the same spot. Again, the joy of the Lord impacted me. Again, I stood there laughing. This was not normal for me, but there was a supernatural event occurring. Soon I continued walking and praying and again, on coming back to the same spot, the joy of the Lord came upon me. The Lord then showed me how to minister in His joy. And exactly as he showed me, the joy of the Lord came upon many of the congregation. I gave out of what the Lord had done in my life, and I had to take the risk of declaring, "God is going to release joy here this morning," with the possibility that I would make a fool of myself.

To add to this, I understand that I am a move of God. Given that John 7:38 states: *"He who believes in Me, as the Scripture said, 'From his innermost being will flow rivers of living water.'"* Wherever we go we carry the river of the Holy Spirit within us, and that river is just waiting to flow out toward others. It is basic to our spiritual makeup that Holy Spirit power is an integral part of our Christian makeup. If we truly believe John 7:38 to be true, then it is obvious that within us is a power waiting for an opportunity to touch others.

This concept is confirmed many times throughout the New Testament:

But you have an anointing from the Holy One, and you all know. (1 John 2:20)

As for you, the anointing which you received from Him abides in you, and you have no need for anyone to teach you; but as His anointing teaches you about all things, and is true and is not a lie, and just as it has taught you, you abide in Him. (1 John 2:27)

We are referred to as the temple of the Holy Spirit. It is therefore anticipated that wherever you go and minister, the Spirit of God will move, not because you are special or specially anointed, but simply because of what God has placed in your life and the lives of believers filled with the Spirit. The key therefore in seeing a move of the Spirit occur in a congregation, revolves around discovering the keys to releasing what God has placed in your life into the lives of other believers.

Determining in My Heart That there Will Be a Move of the Spirit

Faith is the fertiliser that feeds the realm of the Spirit. Faith commences with you, as the minister, making a decision to move in the Spirit, moving until there is a release of the Spirit in a given environment.

One of the ways to look at it is like this: In every meeting there is a treasure to be discovered that revolves around the Holy Spirit significantly touching people's lives. It's like a forest where treasure is hidden. You know it's there, but there is much obstruction, undergrowth and entanglements that must be negotiated in order to reach it. Such obstructions can be:

- Outright prejudice against moves of the Spirit

- Religious conservatism

- Simple misunderstanding as to what a move of the Spirit should look like

- Blatant opposition to anything of the Holy Spirit

- Legalistic attitudes and controls

- Past negative experiences with Holy Spirit orientated ministries resulting in people rejecting ministries that bring moves of the Spirit

- Demonic opposition in many forms such as control, manipulation, demonic deception

- Excessive and extreme behaviours in meetings

I have found the key to dealing with most of these obstructions is clear communication and openness with the pastors and leaders of the congregation I am ministering in. I would not be there if the pastor did not want me to bring a move of the Spirit. As a result, it is assumed that he wants to deal with the issues hindering what God is seeking to do and, therefore, open dialogue between myself and the pastors means most of those types of excesses and attitudes can be dealt with. It is for that reason that I will often request a meeting with the senior leadership of the church I am ministering in before the public meetings commence. It is there we will discuss concerns and the way to deal with them.

There will always be unexpected surprises in meetings. However, through building a confidence with the senior leadership of the church, I am generally able to negotiate my way through some turbulent attitudes and reactions.

So, I come to the church with the deliberate intention of believing for and seeing the Holy Spirit move in the meetings. It doesn't matter how bad the music is, what the attitudes of some of the congregation members are, or the general atmosphere in the church; given that I have the complete support of the pastor and leadership, I will press into having a move of the Spirit.

I enter any church meeting where there is the desire for a move of the Spirit with a vital conviction. There are always two meetings when I come to a church. The first meeting is what happens before I stand up to minister and the second meeting is what happens when I stand up to minister. In an ideal world the two meetings would flow into each other smoothly but, all too often, this is not the case. As previously stated, I cannot be reliant on what happens before I stand up to minister. It is a bonus if the atmosphere I begin ministering from is positive and faith filled, but if it's not, no problem. I stand up and a new meeting has just commenced, which may have little or no reference to what went on in the first part of the meeting. This is not being arrogant; it's simply a way of ensuring that I am not dependent on the atmosphere that is handed to me. It is my responsibility to now build an atmosphere conducive for the Holy Spirit to move.

Begin with a Faith Position

Once the formalities of introductions are over I will then begin by announcing what I believe God is going to do in that meeting. Decreeing what I believe will happen establishes this both in my own heart, the heart of the congregation, and the realm of the Spirit. Faith and expectancy will also be created. Of course some have *heard it all before* and will therefore reject outright what may appear to them as hype. This will rapidly change as the way I move will show a different methodology and one that will win the hearts of the congregation. I will announce what is going to happen with such phrases as:

- Before the end of this meeting many of you will experience the power of God in ways not experienced before.

- God is wanting to touch most of you here today. Be open as He will bring His power to most of you today.

- Many long standing addictions and controls in your lives will be released from you today.

- The Holy Spirit is about to move in life changing ways today.

A number of things are happening in speaking this way. One such thing is that by openly declaring my faith position, I can't escape the faith and fear factors of moving in the Spirit. I can't just retreat behind the pulpit, deliver a sermon, maybe have a weak altar call and go home. No, I must seek to push through into a greater level of anointing and freedom on behalf of the congregation.

But I must also confront the controlling demonic forces seeking to repress the faith and expectancy in the hearts and minds of the congregation. The moment I stand up to minister I have immediately entered an arena of spiritual warfare. The devil, his agents, demons, are certainly going to resist believers coming into spiritual freedom. Such demonic forces include:

- Religious demons

- Controlling and witchcraft spirits

- Spirits of unbelief

- Demons of gossip, criticism and cynicism

- Demons of hatred

Many more will array themselves in conflict to do all that they can to stop or at least hinder me from taking the congregation into a move of the Spirit. They will come in direct contact with me; direct resistance to me. This will often be clearly felt and manifest in many different ways. But by my clear declaration at the beginning of the meeting that the Holy Spirit will move I am, in effect, announcing to them, "Look out, I am unmovable in facing you off and defeating you. I will not be intimidated by the demonic spirits arrayed against me. I am after you and will defeat you! We are going to have a move of God here today!" This is not something I would say outright, as most believers don't understand spiritual warfare and have never realised they are already in an arena of conflict so would have no idea what I was talking about. But the demonic realm clearly understands that I have arrived, that I have come to defeat them, and my declaration that there will be a move of the Spirit in this meeting is an outright declaration of war.

I am stating clearly that I will not be intimidated by these controlling witchcraft spirits. I come to intimidate them. When people come allowing those demons to work through them against me, look out. I will not allow their intimidation to push me down. I will rise above them and have learnt that one of the most powerful ways of defeating these demonic forces is to intimidate them, rather than allowing them to intimidate me. My attitude, clear declaration of confidence and determination, all set up the meeting for the defeat of these demonic forces. My arrival in a church is like an international declaration of war. I am taking the initiative in this war, I have the weapons of mass destruction to kill them off en masse, and I am pleased and excited to push the button.

Most pastors and leaders have very little understanding of this realm of spiritual conflict. It is for that reason they are often ministering for decades, unable to gain the desired momentum and breakthrough, resorting to natural abilities and leadership skills to overcome opposition. This is okay; there are skills that must be employed, but it is fatal to ignore, or somehow pretend, that there are not powerful demonic forces arrayed against the pastor. This is why there is often spiritual and natural upheaval when I go into churches. I come to openly do battle with these forces that have had free reign, often for decades, in a church. My job is to confront, conflict and overcome, which means a battle will occur and there will be casualties in the fight. All too often, the casualties will be in the form of long-standing members of the church rising up in opposition, but their controlling and undermining ways must be exposed and removed.

It will often come as a shock to a local church pastor to see how quickly his normally settled and peaceful congregation suddenly erupts in violent conflict, but confronting and exposing the controlling demons that have lain dormant, but ready for attack, will bring huge conflict and stirrings. It's for this reason pastors should regularly bring into their churches reputable ministries in the area of deliverance, to keep exposing the schemes and plans of the demonic realm. Only then can there be at least some level of assurance that demonic controls operating through people are regularly exposed and dealt with.

It is worth the cost of pain and turmoil. Simply, many things will now be understood such as why the pastor was unable to move the church forward, why unexplained hindrances seemed to often rise up, and why, in his own heart, he was regularly conflicted with issues that were unexpected and unable to be explained. So as my faith position and confident expectancy is clearly established, it is then time to see a move of God.

CHAPTER 2:
THREE ELEMENTS OF A MOVE OF GOD

There are three elements that enable a move of the Spirit to occur. These elements are: faith, gifting and anointing. Closely aligned to faith is also expectancy, but this will be explained further on.

Firstly, we must have some definition of these three terms for the context in which they will be used in this book. Note that the definitions are only in terms of what they mean for bringing a move of the Spirit.

Faith

Faith is the inner dynamic in a believer of *just knowing*, knowing that something is about to happen. It is inner confidence we can have toward a particular area, for instance, healing. Faith is sometimes God-given and quite sovereign, and is spoken of as a *gift of faith* (1 Corinthians 12:9). It is also a quality that grows and develops in our lives, and is called the *fruit of faith* (Galatians 5:22 KJ).

For the purposes of moving in the Spirit, faith may be manifest as a gift of the Spirit but most often, for me, when seeking a move of God it is stubborn determination, based often upon previous experience, but also upon the knowledge that I know God is moving all the time. In practice, it means I will pray for people with a stubborn determination, waiting for something to happen until such time that it does!

Closely aligned to faith is expectancy. This is an important partner of faith. Where there is no expectancy for God to move then it is almost impossible for a move of the Spirit to unfold. Accordingly, expectancy is a factor that must be developed in the heart of the congregation if we are to see a move of God released. Expectancy is built prior to a series of meetings via promotion, but also in the meeting itself when declaration and testimony is given to what God has done and is going to do. With the fertile ground of expectancy in the heart of people, faith will quickly arise.

Gifting

Here I am referring to the supernatural nine gifts of the Spirit as expressed in 1 Corinthians 12. There is a common misconception that we are given some of the gifts of the Spirit, but not others. This is not what 1 Corinthians is saying. When saying: *"...to one is given..."* the reference is to the function of a church meeting, and how to ensure proper order is administered during a public meeting. The principle that overrides all this is stated in 1 Corinthians 12:6: *"There are varieties of effects, but the same God who works all things in all persons."* God works all things in all persons, i.e. all nine gifts of the Spirit working in all believers.

My journey as a Christian has been to work out how to move in all nine gifts of the Spirit proficiently. They are our *tools of the trade* to enable effective ministry into the lives of others. They are, as with Jesus, major tools that are used to effect evangelism. This is evidenced in the life of Jesus when He discerned demonic spirits, operated continually in gifts of healing, and when gifts of wisdom and words of knowledge flowed regularly in His ministry. Jesus gave us this example which we should follow. Not operating easily and proficiently in the nine gifts of the Spirit is equivalent to a builder trying to build a house without his hammer, saw, level, and all the other necessary tools.

Many people continue to be imprisoned in their hearts by past issues that require supernatural insight to unlock the root causes to then see those causes healed. Only supernatural insight will achieve this and that occurs via the use of the gifts of the Spirit. Accordingly, I have made the development of the gifts of the Spirit a major focus, in particular, the gift of prophecy. It became clear to me in my early Christian walk how powerful prophecy, when spoken with accuracy, could be in the recipient's life. Such prophecy would lift the spirits and hearts of the recipients, and bring wonderful encouragement and strength to their lives.

It is beyond the scope of this book to address the problems associated with the excesses so evident in the Body of Christ regarding the delivery of personal prophecy. However, when it is delivered in such a manner that the person receiving the prophecy knows that what has been spoken is accurate and reveals *the deep things of their hearts* then, so often, their lives can be transformed. My heart and prayer for 30 years has been, "God, please give to me accuracy and details when delivering a personal prophecy to someone." Later I will demonstrate why this is so important to bringing a move of the Spirit to a congregation.

The gifts of the Spirit are gifts that can be drawn upon to achieve a particular task at hand. They are not sovereign manifestations of God, but given to the believer to be used as and when necessary to build the work of the Kingdom. We make a choice whether or not to draw on the Holy Spirit to allow a release of the gifts of the Spirit at a given moment. More on that later in this book.

Anointing

The anointing is the power of God to perform an act of God. It is the manifest presence of God. In my previous book, *Increasing the Anointing in Our Lives,* I examine this aspect in detail. However, in the context of moving in the power of God and seeing the Holy Spirit touch people, I make reference to the anointing being the manifestation of the power of God. Of particular note, Jesus refers to an important aspect of the

Holy Spirit in John 14:17: "*...that is the Spirit of truth, whom the world cannot receive, because it does not see Him or know Him, but you know Him because He abides with you and will be in you.*"

This reveals two dynamics of the Holy Spirit moving in our lives: being with us and in us. In a meeting the Holy Spirit will be moving in us internally, within our physical body, and also around us externally, and touching us accordingly. It is this dimension of the Holy Spirit's activity we should be looking for.

Now for the overriding principle that forms the foundation for seeing a move of the Spirit occur amongst a group of people:

> *You, as the one ministering, choose to move in one of the three elements; faith, gifting or anointing, and as the Holy Spirit begins to move through that initial element, the other two will begin to flow, thus increasing the manifestation of the Holy Spirit in that moment of time.*

The following is an example of a typical meeting that may occur that results in a move of the Spirit arising. Imagine the following: I am in a church with a congregation who have not experienced a significant outpouring of the Spirit, perhaps for years. A level of doubt, fear and maybe even resistance is present. Maybe they have been in meetings where there has been too much hype and manipulation, where a ministry has tried to stir something up but there was no reality in it.

There is, accordingly, suspicion and huge levels of caution, yet there is desire present, and secretly the hope that maybe this time something genuinely of the Holy Spirit might be manifest. Perhaps this hope was created prior to the meeting by the pastor since he had previously been in a meeting where I had ministered, so there is cautious acceptance of me though legitimate suspicion.

The praise and worship commences and it is awful. The musicians are poor, the singers cannot sing in tune and the worship leader is just distasteful in their behaviour in leading the music – believe me, this is not an uncommon occurrence. In addition to this, the song choices are poor, often unbiblical in content, and fail to bring the people into a genuine connection with God. In this atmosphere, devoid of faith, expectancy or anticipation, I am introduced to speak, and I stand before a congregation who appear dead, bored and carry an attitude of, "Here we go again…"

I recognise all this, but remember there are always two meetings. The first is the meeting that occurred before I stood up to minister, the second is the meeting that now commences when I stand up to minister. I realise at that point that there is nothing that I can draw from previous to my introduction, but that is okay, as I am not reliant on what happened beforehand.

I share something about myself, family and church in the hope of creating some level of connectivity with everyone. Then I make the announcement: "Tonight God is going to move powerfully in this meeting. Before the night is finished, many of you will experience the power of God in ways you may never have experienced before. God's heart is to touch all of us here. He is a loving Father, and just like a natural father, wants to celebrate and enjoy His children. Many of you here will be freed from long-standing bondages as the Holy

Spirit moves upon you. I believe that before this meeting is over, lives will be changed in powerful ways. Let's be open to what God wants to do here tonight. Let's allow the Holy Spirit to move amongst us in powerful ways."

I will then shift my focus to choosing how I will move in the Spirit. A simple technique that I was taught has profoundly empowered this ability. The Bible explains the dynamics revolving around our natural man and our spirit man. This understanding is partly unfolded for us in 1 Corinthians 2:11-14:

For who among men knows the thoughts of a man except the spirit of the man which is in him? Even so the thoughts of God no one knows except the Spirit of God. Now we have received, not the spirit of the world, but the Spirit who is from God, so that we may know the things freely given to us by God, which things we also speak, not in words taught by human wisdom, but in those taught by the Spirit, combining spiritual thoughts with spiritual words. But a natural man does not accept the things of the Spirit of God, for they are foolishness to him; and he cannot understand them, because they are spiritually appraised.

In simple terms, we have been given a natural man to do natural things. My natural man enables me to eat and do the natural things of life. But clearly to relate to God who is Spirit, I need a spiritual ability to relate to Him. So God poured His Spirit into our spirit, making us one spirit with Him: *"But the one who joins himself to the Lord is one spirit with Him."* (1 Corinthians 6:17)

So now I have a spirit man to do spiritual things and a natural man to natural things. It is beyond the scope of this book to explain this in full and, in particular, how to communicate with our spirit man and accordingly with the Spirit of God. However, I make a conscious decision that I will now sensitise myself and become aware of what my inner man, that inner part of me that God has joined to, is saying and doing. To achieve this I will imagine two circles in front of me on the floor. One represents my natural man, the other my spirit man. I then will step from my natural man circle into my spirit man circle. Obviously I don't do this physically, it is just something I imagine doing. It is simply a way to orientate myself to listen now to my spirit man joined with God's Spirit; to enable a better consciousness of the Spirit of God's voice in my own heart.

Over the years, I have learnt how to immediately orientate myself to listening to the voice of the Spirit within my heart. You may have another way of becoming sensitive to the Holy Spirit's voice within you. It's not the method that is important, but the effect of what is occurring. It's a shifting of your focus from listening to your natural man and voice, to listening to the voice of God, of the Holy Spirit.

All the while, I will be talking to the congregation about *stuff*. It doesn't matter too much what stuff. What they don't realise is that I am now focussing on the leading of the Holy Spirit, listening to the voice of God. How does He want me to move? How does He want me to start?

At some point though, I am going to have to initiate something. As mentioned earlier, I made prophecy a significant focus to develop in my life. I have seen the impact of personal prophecy not only in my own life, but in the life of others. If nothing else, I will make the decision to move and prophesy over someone… but who?

So, while talking to the congregation, I will be quietly looking for the prompting of the Holy Spirit to direct me to the person He would have me pray for. I call this the *omph of the Holy Spirit.* I am looking over the congregation and suddenly I feel an inner drawing to a person, an *omph* inside of me toward someone. I have recognised that this is the prompting of the Holy Spirit as to who I am to pray for, so I invite the person to come forward.

I will explain how to pray for a person so that what is shared is accurate and significantly anointed in a later book. I must emphasise that I have sought to develop personal prophecy that is not generalised, but specific to the person, so that they will come away unquestionably knowing that God has clearly spoken through me to them. As a result, being specific toward them is vital, so I prophesy details of their heart, the past, present and future desires of their heart that they already know. No surprises. The only surprise is that I spoke out things I could not have possibly known, except that God had spoken through me.

Of course, as I am doing this, people who know the person I am praying for realise something supernatural is occurring. They know the person, they know that what is being said is accurate and of God. They are amazed, the person being prayed for is amazed, and maybe even crying, but certainly responding. Suddenly, a shift is taking place in the hearts of the congregation. People are hearing this prophetic flow, and are amazed, thinking, "Maybe he will pick me. Maybe God might speak to me. I am desperate for God to show me that He is aware of me…" So what is now happening in the atmosphere? Expectancy is arising, faith is being activated and with that expectancy and faith, a faint level of anointing is starting to manifest in the meeting. It started with gifting but now the gifting, in this case prophecy, has created a rise in expectancy and faith which will automatically bring to the surface the manifest presence of God, the anointing.

I then ask the person I have just prayed for to report to the congregation immediately if what I have spoken was true and accurate. I'll joke with them and say something like, "If you lie to me don't forget liars will not inherit the Kingdom of God." It's a joke but communicates to them that I don't want them to say it was accurate just to please me; I want honesty. I may even ask congregational members who know them if what I spoke was accurate. At the time of this writing, I am blessed to say that in almost every case of prophesying like this it has been 100% accurate. And for that I give all glory to God for graciously using me.

Now the attitudes of the congregation are shifting. I will continue to now look for another person to prophesy over, and again, as I feel the omph of the Holy Spirit, I'll draw another person to the front and prophesy over them. People are watching and are amazed, but the thing that is changing is that there is an increase in the level of expectancy and faith. And with that rise of expectancy and faith is, similarly, an increasing awareness of the manifest presence of God, the anointing. What is happening? Gradually we are moving together in the Spirit. The Holy Spirit is starting to be manifest in ways that some have neither felt nor experienced before, so I continue doing this for a few more people. Remember, the Holy Spirit is more interested and desirous of touching people like this than we are. We are simply His vessel through whom He is able to touch His people.

After praying for a few people, I come to another person and prophesy over them, but this time the power of God touches them in a dramatic and powerful way. Maybe they are slain in the Spirit; a common biblical manifestation of the power of God where a person is so touched by His power that they are unable to stand anymore and, with catchers on the ready, they fall under the power of God.

Imagine if this is the first time that this has been seen by the congregation. Some will be wondering what is going on. Others may have heard of such a thing happening and secretly wished it would happen to them. I explain that this is a normal and common occurrence when the Spirit of God touches people. But what has happened? I started with prophecy, gifting, and expectancy and faith came. With the expectancy and faith, then came the anointing. Now the anointing is so strong that a person has been overpowered by the Holy Spirit. People are amazed, they are now awake, attentive and expectant. Now they are praying in their hearts, "Lord, please touch me like that!" But what happens now is remarkable. With the rise of faith and anointing the gifting flows and in this case, becomes easier and often more accurate and powerful. But the reality is that I am now in the first stages of a major move of the Spirit. So what do I do now?

Continually being dependent on the leading of the Holy Spirit, I am looking for how the Holy Spirit would lead me to take the move deeper. Maybe I pray for a few more people, the Holy Spirit touches them, and they are slain in the Spirit, but continually there is growing faith and anointing as more people are ministered to. It comes to a point where I prophesy over a person, they get slain in the Spirit, and this is the one that I feel the Holy Spirit directs me to have lifted up back on their feet and to pray for them for the Holy Spirit to touch them, and again they are slain in the Spirit. I have now moved from moving in gifting to moving with the anointing, in other words, flowing with what the Holy Spirit is now doing.

There is a principle of transference and overflow in operation. When the Spirit of God is on one person that can often be transferred and flow over onto another person, and you can use someone who is already under the power of the Spirit to pray for others. After praying for that person three or four times, they will become more and more impacted by the Holy Spirit. Perhaps they can't even stand up due to the increase in anointing on them. Of course, the congregation is fascinated. This is a person they all know and they have never seen them under the power of God like this before. In fact, they may be one of the most unlikely people to behave in such a manner, so they are laughing, the joy of the Lord clearly on their face.

I then have the person held up and get them to choose a friend to pray for. Their friend comes forward. Everyone is watching, wondering what is going on, but all are aware that this is a miracle. The person comes forward, my *helper* puts their hand on their friend and prays, "Holy Spirit touch them." Suddenly, to the amazement of everyone, the power of God touches them, and they are slain in the Spirit. I continue getting other *friends* to come forward. The Spirit of God continues to touch people; people who were often the least likely to respond, but every time they are prayed for the power of God comes upon them.

Now not only is the congregation expectant and faith has come, but the anointing has grown to such an extent that people are being easily prayed for and overcome by the power of God. I continue getting different people under the power of God to pray for each other. The anointing is now flowing all over the congregation. People are now desperate to be a part of what is happening. They can see that God clearly spoke to their friends, and they can see that something supernatural is occurring to people all over the congregation. They want to receive. Where maybe an hour ago they were cynical, resistant and certainly very cautious, they are now hungry, wanting what others are experiencing. It becomes easier and easier to pray for people and see something supernatural happen. The anointing is increasing, the flow of power is increasing, a powerful move of God has commenced!

Now where did this all come from? From a prayer meeting? No! From hyping up the congregation to some fever pitch of behaviour? No! From having someone special and powerful come in to bring this move? No! It was just a normal, average Christian leader! It all started because someone, in this case myself, chose to pray and prophesy by utilising the principles of faith, gifting and anointing. Using one of the elements, in this case gifting, and in this particular instance prophecy, faith came, and so did the manifest presence of God, the anointing. Before long many people in the congregation began experiencing the power of God in ways they had never experienced before.

Now all that is required is some explanation through the preaching; explaining something of why God is doing what He is doing, and what can be expected in future meetings. A move of God has commenced. In subsequent meetings I will reinforce this by further praying for people, utilising the principles of the three elements of a move of God. And now, because the congregation have opened their hearts to what God is doing, it becomes easier and easier to see the power of God released in each meeting. But more significantly, it always increases in power, resulting in significant life-changing personal encounters for the people in the congregation.

Now let's start again, let's go back and imagine the same congregation when I first arrived. Resistant, not free, unaware of the fact that God can and will touch them. I do the preliminaries of introductions, making a faith declaration and so forth. But now, instead of commencing with gifting and as a result prophecy, I look to move with, say, anointing. There is one thing I have learnt over many years of ministering in the Spirit: in most congregations there are always one or two people who are open to the Holy Spirit touching them. They may have kept their love of the Holy Spirit from the rest of the congregation for fear of rejection or criticism, but they can often be easily picked. You can see it in their eyes; a slight sparkle, a life spark within, an attitude. They will somehow display a *yes* as I am speaking of the Holy Spirit touching people, so I will commence with anointing and pray for a few people, believing that on someone the anointing will be displayed or manifest.

Like before, I will talk until I feel the omph of the Holy Spirit directing me to the person to pray for. I will bring them up, and without any long, boring and irrelevant prayers, I will simply pray for the Holy Spirit to touch them and see what happens. Maybe nothing happens. No problem, I will pick others who seem more open to the things of the Spirit, all the time waiting for the person the Holy Spirit will break over. There will be someone, there always is! I choose another person. Remember, I am now moving with the anointing. Suddenly the Holy Spirit overpowers them. They get slain in the Spirit. I have them lifted up, pray for them again and the power of God touches them again. They are becoming increasingly open to what is happening, and as a result, the second time I pray for them is more powerful and impacting. I continue praying for them. I am looking for them to become *drunk in the Spirit*, and quickly they reach that level of Holy Spirit encounter. I now use them to pray for others, assisting them of course. The Spirit of God touches their friends and other congregational members.

Now a move of God is happening. But remember the principle: you move in one element, faith or gifting or anointing, and the other two quickly flow in behind that. So here we are now moving in anointing, but the congregation's faith and expectancy is rising. There is a desire to also be touched, and they are praying, "God touch me as well." The anointing is now building, faith is growing and as I am ministering, the gifting on my life is being empowered. I begin to receive clarity in terms of the word of knowledge, another gift of the Spirit, as expressed in 1 Corinthians 12. People all over the congregation are now under the power of God. I may have encouraged them to pray for the people around them so the anointing has spread all over the meeting, while I am up the front receiving words of knowledge.

I now announce that God is about to heal some people. The word of knowledge is now active in my spirit. I then point to a section of the congregation and say, "There is a person in this part of the meeting and you are suffering from..." (and I will announce a condition I feel the Holy Spirit talking to me about). I will make it specific so that it cannot be just anyone. I may even share when I feel the problem commenced or the cause. Sometimes the Holy Spirit will give me their age, or the time the problem started, so again there is no doubt as to whom I am referring. They come forward and I pray for healing. I ask them how they feel, in particular, percentage wise how much better they are. For instance, if the pain lessened or what percentage of pain has gone. I will get them to share how much the pain has improved. I will celebrate if it has improved, then continue praying until 100% of the pain has gone.

Now faith has come into the meeting not just for the anointing, but now for healing. With the increase in anointing and with faith, the level of supernatural healings grows. The accuracy of the gifts of the Spirit increases so that the words of knowledge become more detailed, increasing the atmosphere of faith and anointing.

Before long, I may move from healing to just praying for the anointing to flow over people.

Soon many in the congregation are drunk with the Spirit. It all started with anointing, then gifting (in this case word of knowledge) started flowing, and now the anointing is moving to such an extent that many in the meeting are drunk with the Holy Spirit. This is all a result of activating the principles of faith, gifting and anointing.

Sometimes I don't feel to commence with gifting or anointing. Let's start again, same congregation, same resistance and lack of faith and expectancy, but this time I feel to start by faith, trusting that anointing and gifting will follow, and a breakthrough in the Spirit will result. This means that I will just keep praying for people until something happens. Sometimes I may have to pray for a dozen people or more; just simple prayers like, "Holy Spirit, touch this person…" Simple faith prayers, where I'm determined to see something break open. Each time I am believing that God will do something in someone in the congregation. After a dozen or so people have been prayed for by faith, suddenly, the Holy Spirit *erupts* on a person. Perhaps I receive a prophetic word or the Holy Spirit just overcomes a person unexpectedly. In either case it was not anticipated. This was hard work praying by faith until something happened but, as a result, anointing and faith are drawn in as God commences moving.

In each case, whether I commence with gifting, faith, or anointing, the other two elements are drawn into the atmosphere. When that occurs, the level of impact increases, as does the number of people receiving a tangible touch of the Holy Spirit. In subsequent meetings I will build upon what has already happened in the previous meeting, reinforcing what people have already experienced by praying for the same, or similar, things to continue. I will then seek to take the congregation further into the things of the Spirit, once they are opened up and breakthrough has come. The result: the church has entered into a move of God.

Yes, God is moving all the time; all the time, God is moving.

CHAPTER 3:
SUSTAINING A MOVE OF THE SPIRIT IN THE LOCAL CHURCH

The challenge, once a congregation begins to experience the Holy Spirit, is how to both sustain and build a move of the Spirit. In the first instance, once the move of the Spirit has begun to unlock in a congregation, there will be a season when the congregation will want to simply bathe in the experience of the fresh move of God that is occurring. The reality is that once a person has received a power touch of the Holy Spirit they will never be satisfied with anything less than that. There is, for them, no going back to what some might say is *normal* church life.

Churches devoid of the supernatural are the ones not experiencing *normal* church life, but they have become so enamoured with a Westernised Christianity, that they have become convinced that their experience of church is the right type of church meeting. However, this is simply not as the New Testament demonstrates.

The New Testament is full of people having miraculous encounters with God, the Holy Spirit doing extraordinary things, and lives being dramatically and radically transformed. A simple example of this is how the Apostle Paul was transformed from being involved with leading the persecution of the early church to one of the greatest leaders and initiators of missions in the early church. Acts 9 recounts the supernatural events revolving around his conversion. A light flashes from heaven, he is slain in the Spirit, he then hears the audible voice of God, he is supernaturally blinded and is eventually miraculously given back his sight.

Yet we settle for something less and create doctrine to justify a powerless church. This is outrageous and effectively robbing our congregations from the potential of what they could enter into if the leaders and pastors just believed and moved in the Spirit. Once the Holy Spirit has begun moving in a church it is important to understand several key factors, such as:

- How to sustain the move of God without compromising other necessary church life dynamics.

- How to deepen the move of the Spirit so that lives are genuinely and permanently changed.

- How to deal with the inevitable opposition that will come from some members of the congregation and even those outside of the local church.

- How to deal with the excesses that will always seek to corrupt a move of the Spirit.

How to Sustain the Move of God Long Term

Building a strong and effective local church is more than just people having great Holy Spirit encounters every time they gather together. There are still the needs of counselling, training, discipleship, teaching, evangelism and outreach, caring for one another and so forth. Too often churches have encountered the Holy Spirit and forsaken all the other necessary church activities, and eventually realise that, though they have had a great time, nothing substantially has been built that will impact and transform their local community.

Accordingly, a move of the Spirit when encountered in a local church, must be properly contextualised in that church so as to ensure people's needs are still met and lives are still cared for. In my own case, the Holy Spirit poured out in 1993 in a remarkable manner. Eventually, in 1994, this move of the Spirit became popularised in what was called the Toronto Blessing. But when the Spirit first came upon us in such a remarkable manner there was no one to pattern off, and we were learning as we went along. Obviously we made many mistakes, but those mistakes gave me the basis from which to train pastors and leaders on the principles that are being shared in this book. In hindsight, I now advise pastors to do a number of things once a move of the Spirit has commenced.

It Is Okay to Have a Season of 'Holy Spirit Meetings' Where Normal Church Life Is Suspended

It is important to successfully build what the Holy Spirit has commenced into the fibre of the congregation. All too often I have heard pastors, when hearing about the move of the Spirit in my church, say something like, "Oh yes we had that once but no longer." It is always said with a sense of sarcasm and superiority, as if to say, "…but we have matured beyond that now!" Very often a church may experience a great outpouring of the Spirit, but after about six weeks it will die down and eventually they go back to what is *normal*. What a tragedy. In reality, what has happened is that the pastor and leaders did not understand what was happening, did not know how to encourage the move of the Spirit, and certainly did not know how to deal with the opposition that came from members of their church as well as the demonic realm.

To avoid this occurring, it's necessary, initially, to have a season where the congregation gives themselves over to the move of the Spirit. Make it clear that this is what is going to happen. It should continue long enough so that not only in the Sunday meetings, but also in the other meetings of the church such as small groups, music practices, leadership meetings and so on, all freely experience what the Spirit of God is doing. At that point, the move of the Spirit now becomes part of the DNA of the church. I call this a foundational anointing. Every church has foundational anointings that were built, at some time, into the very fibre of their identity, and it's important for this fresh move of God to similarly be established as a foundational anointing. For instance, in my own church I may go for weeks at a time without any significant move of the Spirit on Sundays. But at any meeting, at any time, because the move of the Spirit has been built into the foundations of my church, I could stop the normal operations of a given service and open it up for the Spirit of God to move, and very quickly we would be experiencing a move of God.

One of the things the Lord showed me in the early days of 1993 was how the children of Israel were to cross the Jordan river into the Promised Land. They were instructed to have the priests carry the Ark of the Covenant into the river and stand there holding the Ark on their shoulders until such time as the entire nation had crossed over. This is a brilliant pattern for us to follow. Here is the presence of God for all to see. Some will cross over immediately, but it will take time for everyone to get across. And so it is with any move of the Spirit. In secular language we would call it early adopters, mid-adopters and late adopters. Some people will be early adopters, immediately accepting the move of the Spirit and stepping right into the river of God. Some will hold back a little, the mid-adopters, watching, considering is this really *of God*. But, on seeing the effect of the river of God upon the early adopters, they will step into the river and give themselves over to what the Spirit of God is doing.

Then there are the late adopters. They watch, maybe even with a critical attitude. They may not necessarily be against what is happening, but their personality, and maybe their religious controls from the past, cause them to be extremely cautious. And this is okay. As their issues are addressed, their questions answered, and they observe the changes in people's lives, the Holy Spirit will work on their lives and, eventually, they too will step into the river. Time must be given so that the early, mid and late adopters all have a chance to step into the river and cross over into what the Holy Spirit is doing.

Of course there are going to be some people who simply will never cross over; they will never adopt the move of the Spirit. This is a painful moment for the pastor and leadership as once a leadership have agreed that they want what the Spirit is doing, then there can be no turning back. As a result, some people will have to leave. This is a difficult time, as they will often leave with a critical spirit and will seek to defile other members of the congregation with their negativity. However, given that the pastors have done some good teaching on the move of the Spirit and the manifestations, this should be dealt with fairly succinctly. The objective is to give time for as many as possible to step into the move of the Spirit.

To assist the church in transitioning with a move of the Spirit, it is good to bring ministries into the church at this time who have some experience with the moving of the Spirit. Not only can they share regarding what God is doing in other places, and so give confidence to members of the congregation struggling with the move, but their own ministry will add dynamics to the move that otherwise would be missing. It's essential that the ministries brought in are pastors and leaders who have pastored their own local church, so they can advise from a local church leadership point of view.

All too often I have watched as people who do carry a strong anointing and flow of God around their lives, but have never pastored their own church through a move of the Spirit, come in and bring dynamics and teaching counter to what would help to build a local congregation. Yes, people may experience God powerfully, but any move of the Spirit must be more than just having an experience. Even the Holy Spirit's role in all this is to build an effective missional church.

Too many itinerant ministries don't understand the issues a local pastor faces when the Holy Spirit comes and overturns mind-sets, patterns of behaviour, and other local church issues. I want people to advise me who have been there, done that, and can give proven wisdom forged on the experience of journeying a congregation through a move of God.

Giving a season over to the move of the Spirit does not mean preaching, praise and worship, small groups, and so forth, must be suspended. In fact, even during the powerful times in 1993, I still preached every Sunday meeting, and believe that provided some *normalcy* for people during a turbulent period of adjustment.

It is often suggested to pastors to have a season of extended meetings to build the move of the Spirit into a local congregation. The concept being to, over a week or more, to have meetings maybe six nights of the week. I have done this in other churches and have some observations. Extended meetings will bring deeper dynamics to a move of the Spirit, and will enable people who are slower to accept what is happening to watch and decide. My suggestion is to limit the length of time the meetings run, as going for too many weeks can bring too much disruption to normal church life. Extended meetings also invariably attract people from other churches and may take the focus away from what God is seeking to achieve in the local church.

Whenever I have been involved in a series of meetings extending over many weeks, I have suggested a couple of things to put in place.

Firstly, the meetings should finance themselves. Once the offerings fail to cover the extra expenses incurred, it's time to shut the meetings down. God pays for what He does, and if the money is not coming in through the offerings or other means, then it is time to close the meetings.

Secondly, if there is no clearly discernible development and change occurring in people's lives through the meetings, then it is also time to close them down. There is no point in having meetings for the sake of having meetings. I have therefore generally suggested that if there is not a regular flow of new people coming to know Christ, then it is again time to shut the extended meetings down.

Teach the Congregation about the Manifestations of the Holy Spirit

It is a great mystery to me that people can read the Bible, often for years, and fail to see the abundance of people experiencing various manifestations of the Holy Spirit. Manifestations such as shaking, falling over, laughing, being weighed down, and so forth, are frequently seen throughout Scripture. People need to be taught about these experiences in order for them to see that such manifestations are the natural and normal result of a person being touched by the power of God. One helpful comment I have found is to tell people that different people will experience the Holy Spirit in different ways. It is up to the Holy Spirit how He chooses to touch a particular person.

Often the question is asked, "Why, while everyone else is being touched by the Holy Spirit, am I not experiencing anything?" In reality I have no answer to give. I have seen the most sinful person get powerfully touched by the Holy Spirit while at the same time a person whom one would consider the most *perfect of believers* is failing to experience anything of what the Spirit is doing. The only answer that I can give is that there is no reason why one person gets touched and another doesn't. God is sovereign so remain open and keep getting prayer, because you don't know when the Holy Spirit might break over your life.

However, there are some suggestions to help you receive from the Holy Spirit. The most important thing is: surrender. If something starts happening, let it happen; surrender to it. If you start laughing, then laugh. If you start shaking, then shake. Just surrender to what is happening as invariably it will go deeper, and become more powerful, and impacting. A conservative man came into my congregation during the height of the move of the Spirit in 1993. One night, after a powerful move of the Holy Spirit, he came and asked me why nothing happened to him when he was prayed for. I said, "Surely something happens when you are prayed for!" His response was strange. He said, "The only thing that happens to me is that when I am prayed for I lean to the left a little." I suggested that next time he is prayed for and leans to the left a little that he goes a little further and see what happens. At the next meeting when people were being prayed for I saw him shaking dramatically under the power of the Spirit. On interviewing him at the end of the meeting he told me how he was prayed for and leant to the left as per normal, but remembering my suggestion he leant a little further to the left. All of a sudden the supernatural power of God overtook him and he then had a powerful Holy Spirit encounter. This continued for him for years. The point being, he had to cooperate with what the Holy Spirit was doing; to be responsive and open. To be prepared to seemingly make a fool of himself. But the end result was powerful encounters with the Holy Spirit.

Describing the manifestations from past revivals is also very helpful. For instance, one of the things I have often seen when the Holy Spirit is moving in particularly powerful ways, is people rolling on the floor. From one side of the room to the other, they will often roll for extended period of times. I had often marvelled at this, not really understanding what was going on, but on reading of past revivals, this was often a characteristic that occurred.

Many strange things happen to people when the Holy Spirit touches them. Unfortunately, things can happen that don't originate from the Holy Spirit that can bring confusion into a meeting. This can also bring criticisms against what the Spirit of God is doing, so this must be addressed.In 1993/94 many things were happening that I simply did not understand. Though I would often wonder at the genuineness of what was happening, I didn't want to stop what was occurring for concern that I might be stopping something that was a genuine Holy Spirit touch. Accordingly, the Lord showed me:

Jesus presented another parable to them, saying, "The kingdom of heaven may be compared to a man who sowed good seed in his field. But while his men were sleeping, his enemy came and sowed tares among the wheat, and went away. But when the wheat sprouted and bore grain, then the tares became evident also. The slaves of the landowner came and said to him, 'Sir, did you not sow good seed in your field? How then does it have tares?' And he said to them, 'An enemy has done this!'

The slaves said to him, 'Do you want us, then, to go and gather them up?' But he said, 'No; for while you are gathering up the tares, you may uproot the wheat with them. Allow both to grow together until the harvest; and in the time of the harvest I will say to the reapers, "First gather up the tares and bind them in bundles to burn them up; but gather the wheat into my barn."
(Matthew 13:24-30)

The danger? Trying to remove the tares too early and so uprooting the wheat at the same time. It didn't really matter if a few things were happening that weren't the Holy Spirit's work. There is plenty of time to deal with excesses and some of the nonsense that can come with a move of the Spirit.

I learnt to leave some of the negative issues until it became obvious what was the Holy Spirit, and what was simply people being stupid. At the same time, there were often demonic manifestations occurring in the meetings. This is to be expected. The same thing occurred throughout the ministry of Jesus. It was never too long before people started to manifest demonic spirits once Jesus entered a region. The power of God will always bring a reaction from the demonic realm.

The power of God automatically flushes to the surface issues and demonic holds in people's lives, as well as other bondages. Teach this to the congregation. Assure them that just because a few things are happening that are not of the Holy Spirit, that it is not a thing to be concerned about. Explain that we are doing things in meetings all the time that are not *of the Spirit*. Even at times I may say something in my preaching that is not of the Spirit. But so what? We are not Jesus. But are we harmed by this? Not normally. This is just part of our maturation process in the things of God; learning to discern what is God and what is not; learning to discover how to keep the river *pure* from pollutants.

It is also helpful to learn to trust your instincts. In the early days of the initial outpouring in 1993, I held a retreat with pastors and leaders. A pastor's wife came to me and said to me that she had experienced all the manifestations of the Holy Spirit and yet nothing had changed in her. I encouraged her to come anyway, and I would pray for her at some time during the retreat.

What she didn't know was that some months earlier, when the Spirit of God was moving amongst a group of pastors, she was there and I was observing her shaking and falling over under supernatural power. But at the time I didn't feel good about what was happening to her, and quickly picked up that what was happening to her was originating not from the Holy Spirit, but from demons. Obviously, I never told her this. She came to the retreat and I waited until directed by the Holy Spirit to pray for her. The moment I did, she started to violently manifest the demons I had earlier discerned, and had a wonderful deliverance. She was to later testify that as a result of this experience, everything about her life changed; her marriage, her church, and her personal wellbeing.

The question is, how did I know what was happening to her, though identical to what was happening to everyone else, was not the Holy Spirit, but demonic? The only answer is that I had a negative witness, that as I was watching her I was not feeling that inner sense of *yes* toward the manifestations. It just didn't look or feel *right*.

Then there are those who are simply being fleshly, carnal. They enjoy being the centre of attention and bringing a move of the Spirit to focus on themselves, rather than the whole congregation. To discern these people during a move of the Spirit, again, relies on the leader of the meeting being sensitive to the inner witness of the Spirit. Often, people behaving this way can make you feel uncomftable, possibly bringing an unclean feeling around them. The leader may feel that they don't want to look at them, or perhaps it is simply a feeling that something is just not *right*.

During a series of meetings in New Zealand, a woman came in and started laughing. The problem was that it just did not feel right, it was not the Holy Spirit. She was the only one laughing and it was disturbing the atmosphere. But more importantly I didn't feel that the anointing in the meeting at that time was for holy laughter and told her so, and directed her to stop what she was doing. By doing this I preserved the integrity of what the Lord was seeking to do in the congregation. This is a *felt thing*, it's hard to discern. Boldness is necessary to keep order in the meeting, and confidence is required in discerning the current anointing of the Spirit.

The person behaving this way may have been a *good* person, nevertheless, they are drawing attention to themselves and not to what the Holy Spirit is doing. The problem here is that fleshly behaviour, more than anything, will put others off from what the Holy Spirit is doing. It needs to be addressed: however, there is a caveat. Many things can happen during a move of God that the leaders have not seen before, so don't understand. This does not necessarily mean that those occurrences are not *of God*. Caution is required. Therefore, it is often helpful to bring in a ministry experienced in such matters, to help with discerning those things which are of God and not of God.

Seeking God Camps

I held for many years, even before 1993, retreats which I called *Seeking God Camps*. These were opportunities to take small groups of people, maybe upward of 45, away on a weekend retreat, the object of which was to facilitate the opportunity for people to have significant encounters with God. With the outpouring of the Spirit as we experienced in 1993, these retreats became an integral part of enabling large numbers of my church to embrace the move of God. By running three to four retreats a year, I was then able to bring new people to the church quickly into the move of God, as well as reinforce what God had done in the lives of the longer standing members of the church. These retreats proved to be life changing for people, and definitely became vital to sustaining a high level of Holy Spirit activity in the congregation.

The following is the general format:

Friday night: Gather around 8pm – maybe 5-10 minutes of praise and worship (just with guitar).

> Spend an hour or so with everyone speaking in tongues. This facilitates a confrontation of behaviour that will be expected throughout the weekend. It also forces people to focus on God, on how they are feeling, and on their own heart. Then get everyone to write a letter to God. The letter is their expression of what they would like to see God do for them over the retreat. This brings focus toward their desires and what they really would like God to do in their life. Inform them that the letters are confidential, so they can be specific and personal. If they finish their letter early, encourage them to pray over the requests and issues in the letter.

After everyone has finished writing, bring them all back together, with their letters, for corporate prayer. They may worship a little and speak in tongues a bit more, but after a few minutes, have them write their names on the outside of their letter and hand it to a person chosen to hold them all while we are praying corporately over them. I will generally pick a person who I know is open and free in things of the Spirit, a person who will bring an anointing around the letters.

Then, pray over the letters. I start by explaining the following, "These letters contain people's heart's desires and issues. There will be requests for God to bring answers to difficult things. Some of the issues in the letters will revolve around significant demonic controls and bondages that we are going to believe for God to deal with over the weekend. So, as we pray for these letters, we need to be in an attitude of faith for God to bring intervention and miracles into people's lives, as well as stand against the demonic forces behind the many issues."

I then choose a few people who I know are strong pray-ers, who are able to lead a group of people in prayer. I direct everyone to gather around, lay hands on the letters, or the person holding them, or the person in front of them, so that each person has some connection to the letters. I then ask everyone to speak in tongues again, and when I feel the time is right, I direct the pray-ers to lead out in prayer. They understand that they're expected not only to pray for miracles, but to also stand against the demonic spirits associated with the issues in the letters.

They are not asking God to deal with the demons – we are to do so. We cast out demons, not God, as per biblical directives. And so corporately we stand against the demonic issues of control, witchcraft (in terms of manipulation), and of whatever other demonic forces the people leading in prayer may feel led to.

When the praying has finished, the letters are put aside ready for people to collect later. At that point, I will be seeking direction by the Holy Spirit as to what to do. One of the main objectives of any Seeking God Camp is to free people up in the move of the Spirit, so perhaps I will pray for a few people, believing for them to get drunk with the Spirit. I'll then have them pray for others with the objective that most, if not all, of the attendees become drunk with the Spirit. I may prophesy over a few people or do whatever else I feel the Holy Spirit leading me to do. The Friday night meeting will finish sometime between 10-11pm.

Saturday morning: 9am will commence with further praise and worship and speaking in tongues.

During this time I will be looking to the Holy Spirit for direction. During the morning session I may have the people go away to read a passage in the Bible and see what the Lord would speak to them about. Prior to this I will show them how to receive revelation from the Bible when reading it through praying and personalising each verse. After an hour I may get them to come back and share what the Lord showed them, and ask them to pray for each other for a touch of the Holy Spirit. I may prophesy over a number of them, and we may even do some deliverance.

During this time we may even have a Holy Spirit prayer tunnel. This is where everyone lines up in two lines facing each other, while people walk through the tunnel as those in the line pray for the Holy Spirit to touch them. Everyone goes through, peeling off one end and joining the other end to do it all over again. Again, the objective is for people to receive powerful touches of the Holy Spirit: to be freed up in the move of the Spirit.

Saturday lunch: Only for about an hour.

Saturday afternoon: At 2pm we come to what is probably the most impacting part of the retreat.

Everyone is put into groups of four people with an appointed leader. The groups go away together to some part of the facility to pray for each other after I have carefully directed what is to occur. Each person is given a number from one to four. The first person, number one, sits in the middle. The other three pray over them in tongues for at least 10 minutes, no English! They don't necessarily lay hands on number one, but they are praying in tongues with the objective of believing for God to touch and speak to the person being prayed for.

During the 10 minutes of speaking in tongues the three praying will be listening to the Holy

Spirit. What is He, the Holy Spirit, wanting to say to this person? What does the Holy Spirit want to do with this person? After 10 minutes the leader will then stop the praying, and the group then share with number one what they each felt God was saying. Note that I tell them before they go to do this that if they get it wrong that is not a problem. Making mistakes is all part of learning to hear the voice of God.

The three then share. It is inevitable that people who thought that they had never heard the voice of God, suddenly find that what they thought others thought too. They were hearing the voice of God. This is one of the most impacting moments for many people: "I heard God!" Once the group have shared what they felt God was saying, the person being prayed for may then give their response to these things. Again, it is an outstanding moment of honesty, vulnerability and encouragement for everyone in the group. Then number one asks the other three to pray for areas of needs and concerns.

Most Christians have never experienced people praying for them for such a focussed and extended period of time. So now the group is focussing their faith and prayer toward the needs of number one. This process will take a minimum of 25 minutes though, in reality, it is normally 40-45 minutes to just pray for one person. Once number one is prayed for then the whole process is repeated for each person i.e. number two taking the seat and one, three and four doing the praying and sharing.

When all the groups have completed this prayer time, usually somewhere around 4:30-5pm, I bring the groups together to share what God did. At the end of this time I may have them pray for each other again to look for people becoming drunk in the Spirit. By this stage it is getting easier and easier for people to experience the Holy Spirit as the anointing is building in the group and people are letting their protective walls down that so often resist any move of the Holy Spirit.

Dinner time: This is normally around 6pm, though you can never be too certain.

Remember, the Holy Spirit is not constrained by our time restraints. A note here: I always have other people doing the cooking and dishes so that the participants in the retreat are fully focussed on what the Holy Spirit is doing in their lives, and not distracted by other things.

Saturday evening: 7:30pm, or thereabouts, for more praise, worship and speaking in tongues.

Saturday evening is about allowing the Holy Spirit to move as I am directed. I may prophesy over more people, have some altar calls dealing with specific issues as I feel led, have another prayer tunnel, or perhaps have people in different groups just releasing the Holy Spirit over each other. But for the next two to three hours I will be moving in the Spirit with the objective to again have people fully experience the dynamics of the moving of the Spirit. The objective is that by supper time, maybe 10pm or so, people are so encountering God that I can leave them alone in the hall where the meetings are held to continue to experience God in whatever way God is moving upon them. I have often witnessed people remaining there for hours under the influence of the Holy Spirit, seeing things, hearing the Lord, receiving revelation and so forth.

Sunday morning: At 9am we will begin again with praise and worship, and an extended time of speaking in tongues.

> I may send them off alone to re-read the portion of Scripture from Saturday's session for further insight, or to have time praying over their letter to God; whatever I feel led to do. I may prophesy over more people or have further altar calls over issues I feel led to pray into. The objective is to finish around lunch time, between 12 and 12.30pm, so that we can have lunch together. But almost always I will finish the morning session off with a major prayer tunnel and really believe for a powerful Holy Spirit encounter so that everyone is so drunk in the Spirit that their experience will be permanently instilled into their lives.

Sunday night: Back at church, the church congregation are aware that the attendees from the retreat are coming back to pray for people and release an overflow of what the Holy Spirit did over the weekend.

> I will have about six to eight people give a testimony of what the Lord did but, eventually,

the attendees from retreat will come to the front of the congregation and I will again release the Holy Spirit on them so that they become drunk with the Spirit then release them to pray over the congregation. There will always be a major overflow where the majority of people in that meeting will receive significant touches of the Holy Spirit. Why? Because we spent a weekend with a group of people going from *glory to glory*, and with the glory it is invariably going to overflow to others. Thus, my entire church is impacted freshly with the move of God.

Now, for such a retreat to be fully effective, a number of things need to be in place and understood:

- Once registered, you must attend and attend the entire retreat, not just Saturday. This is because what occurs is progressive and built upon what happened in earlier meetings.

- There should be no cell phones, radios, secular music and other distractions.

- All group and corporate prophecies are recorded so that everyone has a recording of the ministry they receive.

- I will always bring with me some mature believers to care for people who may become unsettled or disturbed and need personal ministry.

- Often I will, at various points of the retreat, have people sit with a small group of others who they don't know, to get to know them. This is brilliant for integration of new people into the church.

- I will also bring mature believers who will know how to deal with those who inevitably come who are a little unusual and need careful handling.

- I will always be fully explaining what is happening during the retreat so everyone is knowledgeable, especially when the more powerful manifestations of the Spirit occur.

At the end of each camp, before they leave, I will explain what will happen emotionally to the attendees following the camp. Elijah, following his defeat of the priests of Baal on Mt Carmel, had an emotional backlash where he wanted to die. He never fully recovered from this and eventually was directed to replace himself with Elisha. This was a tragic moment for Elijah, and a significant warning of what can happen when we have pinnacle experiences with God.

I will explain this to the attendees at the retreat, and give them some ideas of how to minimise the emotional downturn they will experience, and so avoid the crash that many have. I encourage them to stay connected to the Holy Spirit through speaking in tongues, keeping worship music playing around them as much as possible, and maybe keeping in touch with others who attended to share their ongoing experiences, and so on.

The bottom line is that I have run dozens of these retreats over the years, and never failed to see dramatic, life changing encounters occur in people's lives. But just as importantly, the retreats have been a major part of reinforcing and empowering the move of God in my church.

Dealing with Opposition

It will come as no surprise that whenever one experiences a move of the Spirit, there will always be opposition. It comes in various forms:

long-standing members of the local congregation resisting the changes and wanting things as they once were, people who think they know more about the Holy Spirit than anyone else and believe they should bring correction, people who just reject outright what is happening as being of God and, of course, people who now troll the internet for what is said about what is happening around the world. Then there is the spiritual attack. The demonic realm certainly does not want the local church to come into Holy Spirit freedom, because then the church just might become effective in its mission as now they are aligned biblically to be a people of power. They might now impact the kingdom of darkness with the Kingdom of Light.

The internet is invasive and, unfortunately, there is always someone, somewhere, out to oppose anything to do with the Holy Spirit and, in particular, the Toronto Blessing. Unfortunately, people read this stuff and listen to it as though the person who wrote it is some sort of expert. But remember, putting an article on the internet does not make that person an expert in anything. People who are busy being used by God don't have a lot of time to write articles defending a move of God on the internet. It can seem that there are more against what God is doing, than for. It is my practice to not even try to defend the move of God, except to people who really matter in my immediate circle of relationships. As for those people writing the negative articles on the internet: I won't read, I won't engage, I won't waste my time over them.

I use one defence for everyone who might question what is happening: *"So every good tree bears good fruit, but the bad tree bears bad fruit. A good tree cannot produce bad fruit, nor can a bad tree produce good fruit. Every tree that does not bear good fruit is cut down and thrown into the fire. So then, you will know them by their fruits."* (Matthew 7:17-20)

In over 20 years of experience in moving with the Toronto Blessing, and other amazing outpourings of the Holy Spirit, I can simply point to the fruit. Hundreds, if not thousands, of people have told me of how their lives have been mightily transformed when experiencing the move of the Spirit.

In churches all over the world, pastors have said, and would even do so today, that their church changed for the better when I came and brought a move of God. Thousands of people have come to Christ as a direct result of the moves of the Spirit through meetings I, and others like me, have conducted. Through some of the amazing moves of the Spirit, I have witnessed, first-hand, great leaders being forged.

Your people will volunteer freely in the day of Your power... (Psalms 110:3)

It is not about me, but the point is clear: I have documented proof, and clearly demonstrable evidence, that whenever the Holy Spirit has moved in the ways in which I have seen and led, these fruit are always evident. I ask this question of those opposing the moves of God I have witnessed: How many people have come to Christ through your negative writings? How many lives can you directly point to who have had long-standing hurts, controls and bondages broken? How many churches have you seen revived in their mission as a direct result of your negative writings and attitudes? How many pastors would say, of you, that their ministry was empowered and revived as a result of your writings? The answer: few if any! Why? Because the error is yours not mine!

Another approach to opposition is to purchase some books by leaders of the moves of the Spirit and, for people who are unsure as to the biblical and doctrinal foundations of the move of the Spirit, give them those books to study. I would suggest you don't waste too much of your time defending something that others have already done brilliantly. Know for sure that the devil will do everything he can to distract you into a defence mode and, consequently, emotionally and spiritually exhaust you dealing with the negativity of people. If you don't go there then soon the spiritual forces will realise this is a trap they cannot ensnare you with and move from that ploy.

As previously stated, some will simply not shift their belief and resistance against the move of God. For some, the time will invariably come that they will move on. For certain, I will not *move on* in order to keep them. I would rather have the move of the Spirit than compromise for the sake of one or two individuals who are stubborn and generally carrying religious baggage from their past. The separation is always painful. It is like a death. However, many have said to me that what they have now is far better than what they had before, so it is worth it, even if that means losing some friends in the process. I truly wish it did not have to be that way, but I love the Holy Spirit, I love the way He moves and I will never allow the religious resistance of people rob from me the freedom of the moving of the Spirit.

However, much more difficult is the spiritual opposition that invariably comes when there is an outpouring of the Holy Spirit. Such attacks can come in many different forms, such as:

- Unexplained fear

- General sense of despair and despondency

- Doubt over what is happening

- Constant replaying in the mind and heart of criticisms that have occurred

- A sense of foreboding

- Attacks by people but they have a power to them beyond the normal

- Unexpected and/or unexplained difficulties and inconveniences occurring

There are many more besides the above list. To overcome these attacks it is necessary to quickly make the call that what is happening in this *incident* is a spiritual attack, so defining and thereby owning what is really occurring. This then empowers you to quickly and with confidence resist the devil and the demons associated with the attack. *"Submit therefore to God. Resist the devil and he will flee from you."* (James 4:7)

This will at times require some strong praying against the demons attacking you such as:

- Spirits of accusation

- Spirits of judgmentalism

- Spirits of hatred

- Spirits of fear

- Spirits of witchcraft, control and manipulation

Of particular note, one needs to be vigilant in prayer and warfare against spirits of religion. *"... holding to a form of godliness, although they have denied its power..."* (2 Timothy 3:5)

Religion speaks the right words, looks right, and appears right, except for one thing: there is no manifest power of God evident. This is religion at its worst. Religious spirits will seek to suppress the freedom and moving of the Spirit. All sorts of criticisms, gossip, and outright opposition to the move of God will come through these demonic forces, of course, via people. But always remember, we are not struggling against flesh and blood. These demonic forces are operating through people, but we wage war in the realm of the Spirit. Standing in prayer directly against these demonic forces is imperative.

Whenever the freedom and move of the Holy Spirit is evident, there will always be, quickly building in the background, opposition via religious demonic spirits. A leader/pastor must take a proactive position, standing in prayer against these demons before they have a chance to take a foothold around a move of God.

It is further suggested that faithful and trusted prayer support people are requested to gather regularly to pray for the church, pastors and leaders, with special focus against the demonic attacks that invariably will arise.

Dealing with Excesses

It is unfortunate but, nevertheless, seemingly true, that moves of the Spirit can attract the more extreme forms of behaviour, bringing disrepute and suspicion to any move of God. Previously the care required in stopping this has been discussed, as it may result in shutting down genuine touches of the Holy Spirit. Yet there are obvious excesses, and simply weird behaviour, that should be dealt with.

When a move of God freshly touches a congregation there is little experience to differentiate between the genuine and the bizarre extremism. Outside assistance in this is often necessary to help make this differentiation. But, at some time, the leadership of the congregation will need to draw a line in terms of what they consider acceptable and non-acceptable behaviour during moves of the Spirit. One caveat however: just because there are bizarre behaviours clearly not of the Spirit, it does not mean the move of the Spirit is not of God. There just needs to be some direction and teaching, with *helpers* trained in dealing with the behaviours that cross the line.

It is difficult to describe what is being referred to here, however, I will share my own experience. For some time, from June 1993 and into 1994/95, I had been taking meetings throughout New Zealand, encouraging what became known as the Toronto Blessing. I was asked to commence support days for pastors and leaders who had been touched with this move, which I did for many years, once a month. I was gaining vast experience in this move, and was relating closely to such ministries as Jill Austin of Master Potter Ministries. She was enormously instrumental in bringing the move of the Spirit to New Zealand and moved powerfully in things of the Spirit. Similarly, I met regularly with ministries around New Zealand who were also very experienced in powerful moves of the Holy Spirit. After some time leading in this move I was looking for the opportunity to receive personal ministry, to further empower my ministry to better carry the role I was clearly called to do. Remember, I had already seen the most amazing manifestations of the Holy Spirit, and renewal all throughout New Zealand.

I heard of a conference in Australia where some ministries were coming from the United States that over 100,000 people had been to, to receive the same anointing. I took this as my opportunity to sit under other ministries with clearly a greater anointing and experience in the Toronto Blessing than myself. I wanted to receive personal impartation while, at the same time, learning how to better move in the Spirit and administer the move of God. What I was about to experience was to shock me, warn me and empower me to protect the move of the Spirit in New Zealand.

Tuesday night, the first meeting, was outside my experience of anything I had seen in New Zealand. I can only describe the meeting as bizarre. People were running around the venue hysterically in what was clearly just fleshly nonsense. They were trying to get me to participate, which I refused, even though I was sitting up the front. I was feeling decidedly uncomfortable. By Wednesday morning I moved to the back of the meeting and witnessed further stupidity, all under the pretence of being the Holy Spirit. The ministries from America seemed to enjoy the behaviour and yet here I was embarrassed, uncomfortable and feeling completely out-of-place.

I think it was Wednesday morning that a woman went to the front of the meeting, placed her Bible on her head, and in a quaint but weird voice, said, "I feel to put the Bible on my head!" Another woman went and stood beside her. Suddenly the first woman said, "Oh, I feel to hand the Bible to this woman beside me." This she did. People were praising the Lord as if this was somehow some great move of the Spirit. I was becoming increasingly disturbed, and yet, I was a leader of this move in New Zealand.

The next thing I knew, another woman went to the front of the meeting and pretended to roar like a lion. This resulted in another eruption of praise as though God was moving. By the evening of Wednesday night I simply did not know how to respond. I was now right at the back of the meeting observing. What I then witnessed was to shock me even to this day. Suddenly, a woman got out from her chair and started running around the outside of the meeting. She then ran from the front up the middle aisle, all the while shouting praise. People used this as a sign to participate either in running, or to erupt loudly in praising God. Control was being lost. Then suddenly someone started crowing like a rooster. This inspired someone else to do the same thing, and some others, again, all in the pretence that this was the Holy Spirit. By now the place was simply weird. Further nonsense continued, all the while I am asking the Lord, "What is going on here?"

Because of certain behaviours of the ministries from America, which I cannot describe in order to keep confidentiality, I had become very concerned. All of a sudden, in almost an audible voice, I heard the voice of the Spirit speak to me, "This is a spirit of self-promotion!" And I could see it. People were drawing attention not to the Holy Spirit, but to themselves. The behaviour of the ministries from America was, similarly, doing the same thing. If there was one thing that I had learnt and promoted in New Zealand, it was that whatever happens to us in a meeting is always to draw people's attention not to themselves but to Jesus. The objective was always to create and inspire intimacy with God. But here people were looking at each other, laughing at each other and somehow drawing from the attention of the crowd to then motivate further excessive behaviour.

Back in my hotel I was now mystified. "God, why did you have me come over here to watch this nonsense? Why all the expense when there was nothing here to receive? Even if I had been offered prayer I would have said 'No' as I didn't want what they had; why am I here?" I soon came to the conviction that maybe there was something there that God wanted me to see, and thereby protect the New Zealand church from and, accordingly, keep the flow of the river of the Spirit clean in my nation. Little did I realise that not many weeks later I was to be directly confronted with the same demonic spirit that I had seen in operation in Australia. I was able to become a significant voice to address the excesses and bring adjustment to a large body of Christian believers and churches in New Zealand.

The story illustrates, however, the danger of excesses and how to recognise this. Clearly, standing in front of a meeting roaring like a lion, passing Bibles from one head to another is, in anyone's terms, nonsense. Making barnyard noises, similarly, has to be questionable. But more importantly than all that, did those things bring attention to the Lord or to themselves? Unquestionably, attention was drawn to those behaving in that manner, and I certainly was not inspired to love God more or to desire greater intimacy with Him as a result.

Here I was being criticised for strange behaviours and excesses in my meetings in New Zealand, but anything that I did and saw in New Zealand paled in the light of what I saw there. So the rule of thumb I understood and adopted was: More of Jesus and less of me. I began to make it plain, "My desire is that when I have left these meetings in your church that your memory will be of what God did and not what Brent Douglas did." I sought to adopt an increasing way of moving in the Spirit that meant I was less the focus; that the Spirit of God was the one highlighted. I know many times I have failed to do this, but the intent remains there. Let God be glorified, let Brent Douglas be forgotten. But the lesson was learnt:

> *One of the primary ways of discerning what is of God and not of God: Does what is happening ultimately bring greater attention and glory to Jesus rather than to people?*

A note here is relevant regarding the *River Junkies*, referring to those people who go from conference to conference, often not committed to a local church. They can become very distracting in behaviour and excess. It is important to keep reminding the congregation that what is being built is a local church under the power of the Spirit, and not just a stop-off point for some blessing.

Altar Calls

The Holy Spirit will move and utilise many different activities during meetings. One of the powerful mediums the Spirit of God can use is an altar call. Used with wisdom and Holy Spirit direction, altar calls can be powerful instruments in deepening a move of God and bringing people into greater levels of Holy Spirit freedom.

It is unfortunate that in much of the Western church, altar calls have become almost a rare occurrence. I was blessed recently when attending a Sunday morning service to see how Pastor Joel Osteen of Lakewood Church utilised the altar call during the service to not only see dozens of people make first time decisions for Christ, but also to powerfully minister to members of the congregation. My own pastor friend who was there that morning went up and was prayed for. There he received powerful personal ministry and prophetic words. He was greatly blessed.

Altar calls provide an opportunity for people to respond and receive prayer. They open up the possibility of people receiving encounters with God that other occurrences during moves of God may not afford them. Altar calls have traditionally been done at the end of the preaching in direct response to the word preached, and this is okay. But there are many other ways for altar calls to occur when a little *Holy Spirit creativity* is employed.

A typical meeting scenario might be as follows: I have moved in gifting, the Holy Spirit is now moving, and people are drunk in the Holy Spirit all over the venue. Things are happening but I can also feel that the move is changing, and I need to respond accordingly. I will be asking the Holy Spirit, "What now?" I am deliberately drawing upon the creative power of the Holy Spirit to direct me. If I feel prompted to pray for people who feel called into youth ministry, I invite those who feel so called, and they come up. I line them up and talk to them about the power of impartation, and that my life is the product of many great men and women of God who have prayed for me and imparted something fresh into my life. So for the next 15 to 20 minutes I pray for them, imparting the Holy Spirit, gifts and anointing to them. What has happened is that I have been directed by the Holy Spirit, of course, but have shifted the focus toward ministry and personal impartation.

It is then conceivable that I could have another altar call, as prompted by the Holy Spirit. This time it might be for healing, in particular, for bad backs. This also affords the opportunity to prophesy over some of these people, bring further ministry to them and so deepen the move of the Spirit. Accordingly, to those learning to move in the Spirit, I suggest writing down a list of say 50 potential altar calls that could occur in a meeting.

Here are a few altar calls that have potential for meetings:

- For healing for specific conditions

- For impartation and empowerment to people called to the music ministry

- For deliverance from a particular demonic condition e.g. depression or fear

- For impartation to street evangelists

- For impartation to those called to missions

- For impartation into different age groups, e.g. those aged between 15 to 25 years old

- For impartation for people called to church planting

- For impartation for a particular gift of the Spirit, e.g. miracles

- For impartation for different ministries, e.g. those called to children's ministry

- For impartation for cell group/small group leaders

And so it can continue. Of course, within each category above there are many different aspects that can be focussed upon. Drafting a list of 50 potential altar calls is easy.

Unfortunately, I have seen the most experienced of ministries make a hash of altar calls that could have been so impacting and life changing.

The following constitutes the keys for effective altar calls:

Focus

When considering an altar call, the first consideration is what result are you, the minister, looking for? How do you want people to respond? All too often a great message is preached, the invitation to respond at the altar is given, and yet no one knows what they are responding to. The obvious consequence is confusion, a lack of manifest anointing and general disturbance now in the congregation. It requires time to prepare for the altar call, when looking for people to respond after a preached message.

What exactly are the people being asked to respond to? Detail this out carefully. For instance, a message may have been preached on faith and now comes the altar call. What I will do is focus the altar call toward, say, those who specifically feel a calling to move in faith in perhaps healing or maybe giving, then pray for a specific impartation of the gift of faith toward that issue.

The anointing of the Holy Spirit seems most effective when there is focus toward a particular purpose. Time needs to be given to considering the focus for the altar call. When there is a lack of focus and people are not sure exactly what they are being asked to respond to, it simply creates confusion. It is essential that the person making the altar call decides exactly what they are asking people to come up for *in detail*. There should be no doubt, confusion or uncertainty as to what the altar call is about. Just asking people to come up for prayer, or for a blessing is never going to release the level of the manifest power of God necessary to bring lasting change to a person's life. Clarity is critical. So when an altar call is being called for, the areas that must be clearly explained are:

- Who you are calling up

- Over what areas

- When they are being asked to come forward

- What will be expected of them or what is going to happen to them once they come to the front

As stated previously, a vital principle to understand is that the anointing best flows when there is focus. Focus also enables the ministry to draw on one area of anointing and gifting, and allow the anointing and faith to build around that focus. What many ministries fail to understand is that when you pray for different areas of need, each requires a different anointing, a different gifting and faith focus. For instance, to pray for healing then suddenly switch to praying for someone's personal needs simply dissipates the focus of faith, anointing and the particular gift of the Spirit that is flowing. Different prayer needs require different spiritual dynamics to enable effective ministry. By allowing yourself, the minister, to be distracted and to pray for different needs, simply means that you never build faith and anointing toward a specific objective.

The problem is often when the Holy Spirit is moving in a specific area and people take this as their opportunity to have their particular need prayed for. Their intention is generally okay but, simply put, they are distracting the focus of what the Holy Spirit is doing. I will never allow other needs to interrupt my flow in a particular area. I will tell them that I will not pray for them just then, but later in the meeting. I also note here that demonic spirits will stir people to interject into a focussed prayer flow in order to distract the faith and anointing. This is a significant tactic of the devil to rob faith and anointing from the atmosphere and it is essential to remain focussed toward what the Spirit of God has led you to do.

To understand the issue of focus and the anointing, think of it this way: you pray for 100 people for healing. What can often happen is that there is little impact on the first 10 or so people, but the focus, faith and anointing is building. Suddenly someone gets healed. Now that healing anointing and healing faith receives a significant boost. Healings are beginning and suddenly someone comes up asking you to pray for their non-Christian husband. Almost immediately the focussed faith and anointing is dissipated. It is for this reason that I will often have helpers with me ensuring such interruptions cannot happen. Some readers may find this thinking foreign, and maybe offensive and hurtful, but done sensitively I have found there is rarely a bad reaction as long as I do fulfill the promise to pray for them later on in the meeting.

Rehearsal and Preparation for altar Calls

As a preacher, how much time do you spend preparing for an altar call compared to preparation for your message? This is a key question when considering that you may be wanting to powerfully impact people's lives at the end of a message via an altar call. If you are going to have an altar call then it should be prayed over and practiced in the privacy of your own home/office. I recommend spending time imagining as though you have come to the end of your message, or maybe you are moving in the Spirit and feel to have an altar call. I would imagine going through everything you would say and do as though you are actually there doing it. Imagine, visualise and rehearse not only calling people up, but *seeing* the people come up, and then visualising yourself ministering to them.

Pray out loud, pray imagining you are laying hands on them; actually do it physically as though the altar call is happening right at that moment. Allow the Holy Spirit to lead you in your imagination, as during this time you will often anticipate what the Spirit of God will do, perhaps receive further direction and maybe even experience the anointing that will come when you actually do the altar call. But practise doing the altar call as though you actually have one occurring right there in your office!

By doing this you will anticipate possible problems, Holy Spirit directives, maybe even prophecies you will be led to deliver over people. You may *see* how many people will actually come up and what will happen but, most importantly, you will have already rehearsed the altar call so you have already *been there* in the Spirit.

Control and Congregational Responses

When altar calls are being called for, and during the altar call itself, the congregation needs to also be kept in focus. Demonic spirits will seek to distract the focus from the altar call. People will begin moving, talking, going to the toilet and so forth. It is outrageous that when we come to the most important moment of a meeting, an altar call for salvation, people take this as their opportunity to move. All that does is distract the atmosphere and interfere with what the Holy Spirit is doing. This must be stopped and churches trained as to what is proper behaviour, especially during a salvation altar call.

It is important to keep the congregation engaged. When speaking to the congregation ensure they are looking at you. While praying for those on the altar call keep talking to the congregation and, as an example, call them to be praying and keeping an atmosphere of faith. When appropriate, share with the congregation some of the miracles that have happened.

Further keys to assist with ensuring the altar call runs smoothly:

- Music: Often the manifest presence of God, the anointing, comes with a particular song. Only have that song playing. *Do not allow the music group to change to another song.* This will change the particular anointing as different songs carry different anointings. Stay with what the Holy Spirit is anointing.

- Altar call teams: Those assisting with the altar call need clear instructions as to what you want them to do. Without that some will use this time as their opportunity to do what they want to do, for instance, prophesy over people. That is okay if it is what the ministry directed for them to do. I generally prefer people praying for those of their own sex unless otherwise directed. Obviously senior leaders in the church are the exception to this. And only recognised and trained people should be used at the altar to ensure proper protocols are adhered to and, thereby, those who have come up to the altar for ministry can feel safe.

- Catchers: In a powerful move of God people are going to be slain in the Spirit and fall over. There must be catchers for every person that is prayed for and the catchers need some level of training, in particular, in how to catch a person and gently take them down to the floor. Personally I prefer men catching men, women catching women, unless previously instructed otherwise.

It is spiritually, and at times physically, dangerous to allow people to pray and minister to people who are either visitors or unknown by the leadership of the particular congregation. I find it helpful to always have a meeting manager who is keeping their eyes out for illicit activity, and has the authority to deal with this or to direct others to so do.

Integrity in Altar Calls

Integrity demands that what is going to happen during an altar call is clearly explained, so respondents know exactly what they are coming up for and how they will be handled. One area I believe is manipulative and outlandish is when someone calls for people who want to give their lives to Christ to raise their hands, but then they are asked to come forward. This was not part of the deal, and the person now feels they have been trapped.

If the intent is to bring them forward then this must be clearly explained when initially being asked to respond. Integrity also demands that if it is stated that something will happen at an altar call, then that must happen. For instance, many times the ministry who is calling for an altar call will say, "I will pray for those who come up…" But the people come forward and then the ministry get the altar call teams to do the praying. The respondents have been both lied to and cheated by the ministry.

If you are going to say you will pray for everyone then, no matter how many come forward, you are morally and ethically bound to do just that, even if it takes all night. If that is not your intention, then tell the congregation before they come forward that the ministry team will pray for them. People are not stupid; they know you, as the ministry, are carrying the primary, and generally most powerful anointing there at that moment, and they obviously want you to pray for them.

This leads to another important dynamic: it is very difficult for the ministry team to effectively pray and minister to the respondents on an altar call with a significant level of anointing. Therefore, I will often first pray for the ministry team, before those on the altar, to empower them to then pray for people.

Further Directives Regarding Altar Calls

- Have the meeting manager position respondents to the altar call in such a way that they can easily be reached for prayer.

- Start praying first for people who are clearly already being touched or appear open to the Holy Spirit. This builds the anointing quickly and easily and allows for an overflow of the Holy Spirit to those who may not be so receptive to the Holy Spirit.

- Teach the ministry team that they should only pray and do to people what they would be comfortable having done to them.

- Don't shout into their ear drums!

- Ministry teams must be taught to only touch people where it is appropriate. Being conservative here is very important.

- When laying hands on people touch them lightly, and under no circumstances should pressure be exerted on people's foreheads, causing them to unbalance and fall over in the pretense that they have been *slain in the Spirit*.

- Keep a vigilant watch for demonic activity in the congregation that would take attention away from what God is doing.

- As the minister leading altar calls, I have often been physically attacked, punched, or had people trying to get to me to pray for me thinking it is a smart thing to do, and so forth. I am not suggesting I have body guards, but it is important to have your meeting manager keep a watch out for those type of surprises.

Rooms in the Spirit

When leading a congregation in a move of the Spirit the ultimate objective is to take them into a level of the manifest presence of God unprecedented in their current experience. One way of looking at this is to enter into the *glory of God*, very much like one sees illustrated in the Tabernacle in the wilderness, Moses' Tabernacle. In effect, the ultimate place of entrance was the Holiest of Holies, the place where the presence of God resided between the cherubim over the Ark of the Covenant. To get to that point the various pieces of furniture in the Tabernacle needed to be passed, each representing an aspect of cleansing and readiness for *entering in*. It is symbolic but affords an effective illustration of how moving in the Spirit can be viewed. There is a glory to enter into but certain aspects within, toward the objective, have to be fulfilled or utilised.

I want to take a congregation into the glory, but to get there we must pass through certain doorways; aspects of the presence of God that deepen our experience of Him, and free us up and prepare us for a deeper level of Holy Spirit impact. Like the Tabernacle, another way to look at it is as *rooms in the Spirit*. Consider a house with a long corridor with doorways leading into various rooms coming off it. Each one of those rooms represents an aspect of the movement and manifestation of the Holy Spirit that facilitates the freeing up of people in things of the Spirit, opening up the congregation to deeper experiences of God. I point out that this is simply an illustration that helps us understand the process of how the Holy Spirit will take a group of people into a deeper experience of His presence.

Let's imagine again a church meeting where there is an understanding that we are open and expectant for a move of God. I begin to move in the Spirit utilising the principles of faith, gifting and anointing, as previously recounted, and choose to commence with personal prophecy. I begin to pick out people from the congregation and prophesy and pray for them. Using the concept of rooms in the Spirit, I have just taken the congregation into a *room*. I remain in that room for a time, prophesying and praying for people.

I sense the anointing building, faith growing and after a while sense the Holy Spirit is wanting me to move on. I am anticipating the time is shortly coming where I need to walk out of that room and enter into another. As a result, while praying for people I am, at the same time, looking to the Holy Spirit for guidance as to where He would want to take us; what room in the Spirit He would lead us into.

Imagine I am praying and prophesying over a person but, while doing that, I feel a joy coming into my spirit. Maybe the person I am praying for starts to experience the joy of the Lord. I realise that the Holy Spirit is now moving the congregation into another room in the Spirit. I then must move from that room, stop prophesying and praying as I have been doing, and begin to move generally through the congregation, praying for people while believing for the Holy Spirit to release His holy laughter. This happens, people begin to experience the joy and, over a few minutes, more and more people start laughing and becoming drunk in the Spirit. While this is happening I am listening to the voice of the Holy Spirit, seeking to anticipate when He, the Holy Spirit, wants me to move from that room of laughter and take the congregation deeper into further dimensions of the Spirit.

Shortly, I begin to sense the anointing is lifting off the joy and I may even have some obvious indicators that the Holy Spirit is moving, such as the commencement of some fleshly behaviour. As the anointing lifts off a particular aspect of Holy Spirit activity people will often try and keep it going but, actually, they move from the

Spirit and into the flesh. I want to cut that off from happening as quickly as I can in order to keep the river of God pure.

So as the joy is diminishing, I am looking for the next room in the Spirit. I sense the Holy Spirit leading me to pray for people, for example, who feel a call to pastoral ministry. I call them to come forward. I am now entering another room in the Spirit, a room of impartation, and I pray for these people. But remember, we are going further and deeper in the Spirit, so the impartation is powerful in the Holy Spirit.

While I am doing this I am asking and anticipating from the Holy Spirit what the next doorway and room is that I should take the congregation into. I soon sense the anointing shifting off the impartation, but notice there are some people who have begun to intercede. I sense the Holy Spirit wants to draw the congregation into the next room of the Spirit, which is corporate intercession, as in Romans 8:26:

...for we do not know how to pray as we should, but the Spirit Himself intercedes for us with groanings too deep for words;...

So I call forth the congregation to intercession, encouraging them to allow the Holy Spirit to pray through them.

Again, this is a deeper and a more powerful manifestation of the Spirit, and people are entering into the Holy Spirit in dimensions not previously experienced. They are powerfully sensing the Holy Spirit. We are staying for a few moments in the room of intercession, but soon I feel the anointing moving. I sense the Holy Spirit is still wanting to go deeper into the lives of people. I sense the Holy Spirit wanting people to experience the glory of God. We are coming to the place that was the objective all along: for people to truly experience the deep things of God and to enter into visitations of the Holy Spirit; visitations that potentially could remain on them for days and days. So I move off the intercession and begin to call forth the glory of God.

Only the Holy Spirit can do this; I can't! All I am doing is being led by the Holy Spirit as to how He is wanting me to move and lead the congregation. With great marvel I watch as the Holy Spirit begins to powerfully impact people with His glory. When the Bible speaks of the glory of God it is translated from the Hebrew word *weight*. Accordingly, people are literally under the *weight* of the Holy Spirit. We are now in the room of the glory of God. It is there I may feel to stay or, when I feel the Holy Spirit lifting off that dimension, to then move into some praise and worship and close the meeting.

The whole journey may have taken an hour, maybe two. What has happened is that people all through the congregation have experienced dimensions of God's presence and anointing that have now empowered them, inspired them, and certainly opened up to them the reality that there are deeper and more lasting things of the Spirit to experience than they could ever have thought possible. But for the church, it is now becoming truly empowered with the Holy Spirit and ready to take the mission of the Kingdom of God further because now they have entered into Holy Spirit power.

CHAPTER 4:
USING THE FIVE PHYSICAL SENSES

Essential to moving in the power of God is understanding how the Holy Spirit works with us to enable us to know what He, the Holy Spirit, is doing and wanting to do at any given moment of time. The key to this is recognising that the Holy Spirit works with our five natural senses; touching, hearing, tasting, smelling, seeing. Each of these five senses can be impacted by the Holy Spirit, thus leading us toward what He is wanting to achieve.

… who because of practice have their senses trained to discern good and evil. (Hebrews 5:14)

We need to train our senses to be sensitive and discerning in terms of what the Holy is doing. In doing so, we can quickly see God's power released in situations we are ministering into. The Greek word for "senses" means *organ of perception*. It is derived from a word meaning: to perceive by the bodily senses and with the mind. The result is that the Spirit of God uses our five natural senses to enable us to discern what the anointing of the Spirit is doing.

Let's look at each of the five senses and discover how the Holy Spirit often works with them.

Hearing

In particular, hearing the voice of God. We must know the voice of God as, no matter what the Holy Spirit is doing, that is eventually communicated to us via His voice. I can often can feel the anointing, sensing that God wants to move and yet not know what to do. I therefore have to hear the directives from the Holy Spirit.

It is easy to hear the voice of the Holy Spirit. The key to hearing is that when under the influence of the Holy Spirit, generally, what we initially hear is of the Holy Spirit. The problem is that we have often been conditioned to think it's hard to hear His voice; that only specially anointed ministries can really hear the voice of God clearly and so, through fear and doubt, we question if we have heard God. It is important to trust those initial promptings.

The mistake is to think that God speaks to us in the same way another person does. The idea of a flowing conversation where we are saying one thing and then God responds by saying something, and then we ask Him a question and He immediately answers us, is simply not the way His voice comes to us. Unfortunately when, say, a preacher, shares something he feels God has spoken to him about, he communicates this as coming to him in a conversational style. Though that's easy way to share what the Lord said, it really is not the way it occurred.

The voice of the Spirit generally comes as either a flash thought, flash idea or flash picture that comes to our *mind's eye*. It comes to us quickly, as a short impression or thought. The key then is to *capture* those initial thoughts, flash ideas and pictures. Then, as we meditate on those thoughts and maybe pray over them, further thoughts, pictures or ideas will come to us. Over a period of time, while this is happening, we develop an understanding of what God is saying as those thoughts, ideas or pictures start to come together. A way of illustrating this process is to describe how the gift of prophecy will often work. The following is a description of what can often happen, and the way the voice of God works: Say, for example, I am about to prophecy over a person. A flash thought comes to mind:

Lover of people.

I think about that for a moment, and then another thought comes to mind:

Heals the broken-hearted.

I think on that for a few seconds, and a picture flashes to my mind's eye:

House with broken, hurting people coming to it.

Then another flash idea comes to mind:

Rejoicing people healed.

So, putting that together, I would be saying in a prophecy to the person:

"I see that you are a person who is lover of people.

Your heart is to see the broken-hearted healed. And I see that God has put on your heart a desire to have a house where broken and hurting people can come to find healing. I see that people leave rejoicing because you provided a place for them to find healing for their inner pain."

Of course, in a church meeting context the way this flows is that each flash thought simply flows from one thought to another. As I share each thought, idea or picture, quickly the next one follows, so a flow develops. But what is vital to understand, is that it all comes from these flash thoughts, pictures, or ideas. As we gain confidence in this process, the flow becomes easier and quicker, it's not a conversational style of communication.

The question often asked is how do we know if what we are seeing or hearing is the Holy Spirit, and not just our own mind and thoughts? The answer is: through experience and learning to link what we are hearing with the inner confirming of the anointing of the Spirit within us. This is where the next aspect of our senses comes in: our feelings. Having said that, it is important that we allow people to make mistakes in what they hear. We learn by our mistakes. What we heard, and maybe shared, as being not *of God* is okay. We are all learning, and those that would be critical of this are simply demonstrating a religious, restrictive control that inhibits a learning environment. And to be honest, I practise hearing the voice of God. Perhaps while I am talking to someone I'll ask the Lord what He might want to say to them. I will share those thoughts in such a way that they don't know what I've been doing in seeking to hear God on their behalf. If what I have heard is God, the recipient will witness to this, and more often than not, say something confirming that I had heard God.

Feelings

Our feelings, both inner emotional responses and physical feelings, are vital to discerning what the Holy Spirit is doing and saying. In many respects, our feelings are the gateway into the anointing and flow of the power of God. What we physically and emotionally may feel enables us to discern what the Spirit is doing. I will demonstrate shortly the critical partnership between hearing and feelings, but for this to work, we need to learn to receive the anointing and power of the Holy Spirit freely.

One of the most important principles in moving in the Spirit and releasing the anointing around our lives, is the principle of surrendering or yielding. For instance, we are in a meeting and begin to *feel* something. We may start swaying, laughing, maybe crying a little or even trembling or shaking. Our immediate response is to take control, stop those reactions, hold back and regain our composure. In certain circumstances, obviously, this should be done. But there are times when it is appropriate to surrender to these responses, for example, when we are in a Holy Spirit type meeting where such manifestations are encouraged, or at least allowed. In surrendering, the physical or emotional responses will increase and become more powerful. Our sense of the presence of God will, accordingly, be significantly increased. In reality we are enabling ourselves to gain greater access and experience of the Holy Spirit.

There are many people who do not like this type of behaviour, but I am not writing to such people. I am writing to people who desire a genuine and powerful encounter with the Holy Spirit. From the beginning of the Bible right through into the New Testament there are clearly demonstrated examples of physical manifestations people experience when the Holy Spirit touched them. My suggestion to people who resist this idea of physical manifestations of the Holy Spirit is simply, "Read the Bible."

As people learn to *yield*, and experience the various manifestations of the Holy Spirit, they become increasingly familiar with the way the Holy Spirit touches them and learn quickly to respond to the promptings of the Spirit. They will soon learn that they don't need to always surrender so fully, but respond to the initial promptings of the Spirit that come on them physically or emotionally and then minister to others from those experiences. These physical responses are our way of responding to the anointing. For each person it is different, but it's those physical and emotional reactions that assist us to know what the Holy Spirit is doing. The more familiar and comfortable we become with these responses, the greater the access we gain to the realm of the Holy Spirit.

We have always experienced powerful Holy Spirit encounters in our church. It has been encouraged, and Sunday nights, in particular, have often been the place to fully experience the manifestations of the Spirit. The story mentioned earlier about the man who came in to church hungry for the Holy

Spirit to touch him, thinking that something was wrong with him because nothing ever happened, is simple, yet profound, as embodied in it is one of the great keys to experiencing the power of God: yield! He had heard me sharing at a meeting about the the importance of yielding to whatever they were sensing, no matter how slight. Once he chose to yield, the supernatural power of God overtook him, and he freely experienced the moving of the Spirit for years to come.

There are two aspects to the *feelings* side of the move of the Spirit: the inner anointing and the external, or physical, anointing.

The Inner Anointing

This is where the Holy Spirit touches us on the level of our emotions and our human spirit that, as a believer, is joined to God's Holy Spirit. *"But the one who joins himself to the Lord is one spirit with Him."* (1 Corinthians 6:17)

When the Holy Spirit touches us at this level we may feel:

- An inner quickening

- An inner assurance

- An inner confidence

- An inner conviction

In other words, within us the anointing comes and brings a sense of *this feels good*, or, what I am doing *feels right*. Put another way, we may believe that we are being lead by the Holy Spirit to do something and, given that it is of God, it will be accompanied by this inner witness. We will feel an inner assurance, "This feels right!" Colossians 3:15 speaks of the Holy Spirit being our umpire, meaning that there will be an inner *yes* in our hearts if what we are feeling the Spirit of God is leading us in is, indeed, His will.

And let the peace (soul harmony which comes) from Christ rule (act as umpire continually) in your hearts [deciding and settling with finality all questions that arise in your minds, in that peaceful state] to which as [members of Christ's] one body you were also called [to live]. And be thankful (appreciative), [giving praise to God always]. (Colossians 3:15 Amplified Bible)

This inner anointing will often come to us as a sense of expectancy and excitement within, or we may suddenly experience a heightened awareness; an extra sensitivity of the atmosphere around us. Elizabeth experienced this when the baby leaped in her womb on contacting the presence of Jesus in Mary's womb; there was a *leaping within.*

When Elizabeth heard Mary's greeting, the baby leaped in her womb; and Elizabeth was filled with the Holy Spirit. (Luke 1:41)

So, to describe how this may work, when I am listening to the voice of the Holy Spirit and believe I have heard a word, the question that helps me decide if that word is from God or not is the inner witness I feel. Do I feel an inner quickening, assurance, confidence, or conviction? Do I feel that inner sense that what I am hearing *feels good, feels right?* Do I feel an inner sense of peace that what I am hearing is, indeed, from the Holy Spirit?

When I feel something from the Holy Spirit I will frequently have, in my heart a sense of expectancy, excitement; a leaping within. The result is that whenever I am being lead by the Holy Spirit I am, at the same time, listening to my inner man. Do I have that inner witness, *this is of God?* And I will discern that inner witness as described above.

Other feelings I may have when the Holy Spirit is moving upon me can be sensing a change of atmosphere in the meeting. For instance, suddenly I may feel:

- A deep peace

- Or a great love for people

- Maybe a sudden sense of holiness

- Or a feeling of freedom, joy and freshness

When these changes in atmosphere occur, this is the way the Holy Spirit will tell me that the direction of the meeting needs to change. For instance, maybe we are enjoying the praise and worship and, I suddenly feel an inner sense of great love in the atmosphere. Therefore, there is a high likelihood that the Holy Spirit wants to bring His love to the congregation in a special way. I will then be asking the Lord what it is He wants to do regarding His love for people. It could be that He might lead me to bring people forward to pray for those who have trouble sensing or knowing the love of God, or that I just need to talk to the congregation for a few seconds concerning how much God loves them, encouraging them to open themselves up for a special impartation of the love of the Father in heaven.

In the same way, I may feel a joy has come into the atmosphere. Then I might be led by the Holy Spirit to change the service and open it up for people to experience the joy of the Lord.

One particular inner anointing that I often feel is what I refer to as an *inner burdening*. The best way to describe this is as though I'm almost out of breath and need to breathe deeply. When this happens I have come to understand that, for me, it means a prophetic anointing has come upon me for revelatory gifts to operate such as prophecy or words of knowledge. I have learnt to associate various *feelings* with particular directions that the Holy Spirit would like me to move into. Note that for each person it is different. Just because I might feel that this inner burdening is a directive for me to move into prophetic ministry, it does not mean that this would be the case for others who might receive this type of anointing. Each person must learn for themselves what various manifestations of the Spirit mean for them.

A further feeling, which will often come upon me is, suddenly in a meeting, having a sense of being 10 feet tall and almost floating off the ground. Obviously this is not literally happening, but I have a sense as though it is. For me, I have come to understand this to be an anointing for praying for people for deliverance from demons. I will then move the meeting into deliverance.

Other inner anointings that I have experienced can be described like this: A nervousness that's not really nervousness in the normal sense of the word, but a sense of tension where I feel *arrested* by the Holy Spirit. Or I may feel a sense of empathy or identification with the person I am praying for. This may manifest in me, for example, by feeling the same grief as they are feeling, thus enabling a more sensitive time of prayer and ministry and assisting me in defining what is really happening in their heart.

All these inner anointings simply are the Holy Spirit's way of leading me into what He wants me to do.

The External or Physical Anointing

There are physical things you may feel when the anointing is moving on you. You may feel such things as:

- Heat or moving of heat where your body temperature seems to rise significantly

- Tingling over parts of your body

- Shaking

- Shivering

- Swaying, which may lead to drunkenness

- Physical weighing down

- Jerking

These are common manifestations experienced by people when the Holy Spirit comes upon them. As stated previously, in the early stages of learning to move in the Spirit it is important that you surrender to these physical responses and allow them to actually build, in order to become familiar with these types of manifestations. As you mature you learn to focus these physical anointings toward the objective you have in ministry or prayer. It is difficult to pray for a person if you are jerking or falling over, so you learn to focus these anointings so as not to distract people, but most importantly, to bring the anointing you are feeling toward the objective of your prayers.

A good illustration of this is when you have a powerful fire hose squirting water. If it's not held tightly and directed toward the fire it will simply flap everywhere and be virtually ineffective in putting the fire out. But by taking control and directing the water, the fire is extinguished. And so you learn to do this with the anointing that comes upon you. This leads us to understand that there are times when we are in a *receptive mode* for the purpose of refreshing and empowerment and we just let it happen and surrender. But when we are in a *giving out* mode, we learn to focus the anointing toward the objective.

Now, why these physical manifestations? They tell us that God is here; the Holy Spirit is moving. They will come upon us in order to confirm that what we have *heard* from the Holy Spirit is indeed of the Spirit. When we hear from the Spirit, the inner and/or physical manifestations enable us to have confirmation that what we are hearing is *of God*.

Some people will say that moving in God is not according to feelings but according to faith. This is simply an incorrect understanding. It is both faith and feeling. By combining the two we are greatly empowered to move in the ways of the Holy Spirit. Feelings are essential to sensing and knowing what God is currently doing. Many times we may sense the anointing in a meeting, as described above, but nothing further happens. Yet the Holy Spirit is so close and ready to move. The Holy Spirit is actually trying to lead us. Accordingly we must learn to respond to what we feel and link this with hearing what the Holy Spirit wants to then do. We link hearing with feeling. Maybe as we are feeling the Holy Spirit all we say is, "The Holy Spirit is here in a special way." And this may be enough to release further flows of the Spirit of God. Significantly, people who are also feeling similar things will now be affirmed that what they are feeling is of the Spirit, and so faith and expectancy will arise. This is always a key to experiencing a move of God.

Often the Holy Spirit will link certain feelings or anointings with particular things He wants to do in a meeting, so what you are feeling is actually a directive to move in a certain way in the Spirit. The problem so often seen in meetings is that these things happen, but are ignored by the person in leadership of the meeting. Often they are ignorant of the ways of the Spirit, so a potential move of God is missed simply because they did not understand that these feelings are the manifestations of the Spirit to bring something fresh into the environment.

Seeing

As mentioned above, the Holy Spirit will often bring pictures into our *mind's eye*. This refers to our imagination where we *see* pictures. They come as flash pictures that are suddenly there in our imagination The key here is to be open and aware of what you are seeing and pull those pictures forward into your consciousness. You *see* but then it is important to hold on to those pictures. Obviously this is an area that requires linking with the inner witness of the Spirit. People have vivid imaginations that are not necessarily from the Holy Spirit so, again, the aspect of feelings is linked with seeing. Via our imagination and visualisation, when quickened by the Holy Spirit, we are enabled to see into the spirit realm.

I will often close my eyes and *look* into the spirit realm over a person's life or over a church, believing for the Holy Spirit to show me things. I will deliberately try to *see* what is happening there. I will do this when I sense the anointing. Often before a meeting, having been in prayer, I begin to sense the anointing and so will ask the Holy Spirit to show me what He wants me to do and then actually in my mind's eye *see* that happening. Then when I go the meeting I will simply do what I had previously seen in prayer. This is a biblical way of operating in the Spirit:

Therefore Jesus answered and was saying to them, "Truly, truly, I say to you, the Son can do nothing of Himself, unless it is something He sees the Father doing; for whatever the Father does, these things the Son also does in like manner... (John 5:19)

Often when moving in the prophetic I will get pictures and impressions about a person's past, their ministry, family and so forth. These are powerful tools enabling me to more effectively minister to the person. Alongside of this is the ability to actually physically see things that the Holy Spirit reveals. For instance, I often will actually see the demonic spirits on a person's life. For me it will generally be revealed as a dark shadow over a person's eye.

In the early days of learning to move in the Spirit I would often see the light in an area of a building shimmer; it seemed to *diffract*. After talking to experienced Holy Spirit ministries I came to understand that this was actually the effect that the presence of angels had in a meeting. The lesson is to keep your eyes open to see what the Holy Spirit might reveal to you.

I learnt through boating in the dark that one of the ways to see what is in front of you is via peripheral vision. Interestingly, in recent times science has understood that our peripheral vision is very powerful. It is via my peripheral vision that I will often initially physically see demons on people.

I am also aware of seeing people and their demeanour, attitude, their appearance. I look at a person and they may look: bitter, angry, peaceful, disturbed and so forth. This perception is important to helping me understand where a person is at in their heart. Is this from the Holy Spirit or simply a natural observation? I am not sure, but what I do know is that the Holy Spirit empowers my level of sensitivity and awareness of these aspects.

Smelling

The Holy Spirit will use our sense of smell to discern what He is doing. Very often we will smell the fragrance of the Holy Spirit. A perfume will often come into a meeting. For some this fragrance will come as a whiff while for others it will come and remain on them for a period of time. Often when this manifestation of the Spirit comes it's accompanied by a very deep awareness of the closeness and intimacy of the Lord.

I have learnt to wait on the Lord when this happens. In doing so, the fragrance will increase and more people will begin smelling it. I will ask who is smelling the fragrance, then wait a bit longer and ask again. Frequently, more people will indicate that they can smell it. It is not unusual for 90% of a congregation to smell the fragrance of the Holy Spirit; many for the first time. And why would the Holy Spirit do this? Simply to encourage people!

But we can also smell the presence of demons. Often I will walk past a person and smell a foul, rotting stench. It normally signifies the presence of unclean demons on the person. The amazing thing about this aspect is that I will often smell this horrendous smell, while the people around can't smell anything. It is a discerning of spirits and vitally important to assist me in knowing what is going on at a given moment, either in a meeting or a person's life.

Tasting

This is one of the unique and amazing manifestations of the Holy Spirit. Often when the Holy Spirit is moving in a particularly powerful way people will taste a physical sweetness on their tongues; like a sweet powder. This, again, just helps me know that the Holy Spirit is present in a powerful way and, no doubt, there are other things the Holy Spirit will now want to do. But again, I have often had a foul taste suddenly come into my mouth. This is a discernment of demonic spirits. By linking this with seeing, hearing and feeling, I will have confirmed what the Holy Spirit is wanting to do.

Finally, why are all these things important? The five senses, when utilised by the Holy Spirit, simply confirm His presence and moving, and release us into greater dimensions of the Spirit. By learning how to respond to the five senses when touched by the Holy Spirit, the realm of the anointing is unlocked. When we respond to these anointings the Holy Spirit is honoured and will, correspondingly, release His power to us in greater ways.

So often we cry out for a move of the Spirit, hoping one day something greater will happen. However, the truth is that these things are happening all the time in people's lives. The key is to respond and not ignore the anointings and manifestations of the Holy Spirit. When the Holy Spirit knows and trusts that we will no longer ignore Him when He does come, He will release more to us.

Bringing this together, I want to focus on how this occurs when praying for a person. The keys are:

- What do you sense around them?

- What do you see on or in them?

- What is their demeanour or appearance?

- What pictures, flash thoughts or impressions do you have concerning them?

We learn to be aware of what we are feeling and sensing around the person. The key then to discernment is putting words to what we feel, sense and see. This takes time to learn, and mistakes will be made, but it's a journey well worth taking. Through allowing the Holy Spirit to lead you in this manner, lives will be impacted and changed. When we link this understanding of how the Holy Spirit uses our five senses with moving in the Spirit and bringing moves of God to a congregation, we are greatly empowered to be more effective and impacting.

CHAPTER 5:
GOD IS MOVING, NOW WHAT?

A Move of God and Church Life

The Holy Spirit moves and, as normal, everything is shaken up. People's conservatism and religiosity is challenged and the systems of the church are often stretched. How does a local church operate long term under a move of the Spirit? What issues will they face and how will they deal with them?

The shock comes when a local church has an amazing and life changing encounter with the Holy Spirit, then they discover that moves of the Holy Spirit don't automatically equate to the church growing. In fact, more often than not the church loses people, at least initially. One of the reasons for losing people is that a move of God will change many of the dynamics of the local church, such as the style of services, the type of music necessary to undergird the move of the Spirit, and they may just not like the manifestations of the Spirit. The church is no longer the same as when they joined, so instead of changing with the move of the Spirit, the church member leaves.

Alongside of this, often the leadership will disconnect. Everything was okay when nothing much was happening, but suddenly there is an outpouring of the Holy Spirit and opposition comes. The leaders are faced with angry, critical people, not to mention the spiritual opposition now being experienced. Of course this is New Testament Christianity with all this opposition happening, but that is not what they signed up for when they agreed to be in leadership. They simply don't have the tenacity of spirit and faith orientation to stand in the day of battle. Spiritual warfare had been, for them, some Bible study, but to suddenly find themselves in the midst of war, well that wasn't part of the deal. As a result, they become a modern example of Psalm 78:19: *"The sons of Ephraim were archers equipped with bows, Yet they turned back in the day of battle."* Yes, leaders equipped with all the teaching, but the battle finally arrives and they cannot stand.

This forsaking of congregational members then raises another issue: "The churches down the road are bigger without this Holy Spirit stuff, so what is happening can't be God!" And indeed it does often seem that churches who embrace moves of the Spirit such as the Toronto Blessing don't seem to grow. But then using the lack of church growth as a determining factor of whether the move of the Spirit is of God or not, is simply erroneous. The book of Acts demonstrates moves of the Spirit and incredible church growth. The issue, therefore, is not the validity of the move of the Spirit, rather how we, as leaders, handle the move and pastor our churches through it.

What is necessary in a church that experiences a move of the Spirit is, yes, embrace the outpouring of the Spirit, but ensure to keep alive the mission and the structures of the church to ensure a strong local church is upheld. In fact, a move of the Spirit has the potential to enormously empower the mission of the church, and ultimately bring church growth. Alongside a move of God, there are certain other aspects of church life that need to be upheld, to help a good church remain a good church. People also need certain understandings to enable them to walk through the up and downs of a move of God.

Focus the Congregation on the Purpose of the River of God

Then he brought me back to the door of the house; and behold, water was flowing from under the threshold of the house toward the east, for the house faced east. And the water was flowing down from under, from the right side of the house, from south of the altar. He brought me out by way of the north gate and led me around on the outside to the outer gate by way of the gate that faces east. And behold, water was trickling from the south side.

When the man went out toward the east with a line in his hand, he measured a thousand cubits, and he led me through the water, water reaching the ankles. Again he measured a thousand and led me through the water, water reaching the knees. Again he measured a thousand and led me through the water, water reaching the loins. Again he measured a thousand; and it was a river that I could not ford, for the water had risen, enough water to swim in, a river that could not be forded.

He said to me, "Son of man, have you seen this?" Then he brought me back to the bank of the river.

Now when I had returned, behold, on the bank of the river there were very many trees on the one side and on the other. Then he said to me, "These waters go out toward the eastern region and go down into the Arabah; then they go toward the sea, being made to flow into the sea, and the waters of the sea become fresh. "It will come about that every living creature which swarms in every place where the river goes, will live. And there will be very many fish, for these waters go there and the others become fresh; so everything will live where the river goes. And it will come about that fishermen will stand beside it; from Engedi to Eneglaim there will be a place for the spreading of nets. Their fish will be according to their kinds, like the fish of the Great Sea, very many. But its swamps and marshes will not become fresh; they will be left for salt.

By the river on its bank, on one side and on the other, will grow all kinds of trees for food. Their leaves will not wither and their fruit will not fail. They will bear every month because their water flows from the sanctuary, and their fruit will be for food and their leaves for healing." (Ezekiel 47:1-12)

The house (or temple) is representing the church. The river is representing the flow of the river of God, the Holy Spirit. The first thing that is overwhelmingly obvious is that the further the river gets from the temple, the church, the deeper it becomes. In other words, when we take the river outside of the walls of the local church it will increase in flow and power. It is my conviction that the Charismatic movement made a fatal mistake by allowing the movement to become very much about the church and not about transforming our society and communities. Wonderful things were happening but, very quickly, it became about the wonderful church meetings, the worship, the gifts of the Spirit being utilised to bless each other and so forth. It is no wonder the souls didn't get saved that should have. It is no wonder that 15 or so years into the Charismatic movement it was losing its power and refreshing aspects.

The Prophetic movement had the same fatal flaw to it. The late 1980s and 90s saw this incredible move of the prophetic come to the church. I was significantly involved in this, and well remember the amazing meetings, the move of God and prophetic flows that were unlocked. But again, it never touched the local communities. Instead, it became about paying your $120 conference fee and you would be guaranteed a three minute prophecy recorded on a tape. I am ashamed now to admit that I bought into this for a season, but soon recognised how corrupted this valid move of God had become. I thank God for those Christian leaders around the world who began to voice the need to take the power and gifts of the Spirit out into the community and become a redemptive force.

But the lesson is clear. A move of God is about empowering the local church to better address the needs of the community. It is for that reason the prophet Ezekiel, while enjoying the river and all the refreshing that came with it, is suddenly interrupted: *"He said to me, 'Son of man, have you seen this?' Then he brought me back to the bank of the river."* (Ezekiel 47: 6) This was the most profound of moments. He was told to get out of the river, get up on the bank and see where the river was going and what it was achieving. And the shock of what he saw? The river was healing the bitter tasting water, living creatures were coming alive, there were many fish and great fishing. Oh yes, a few places were not being affected, but then he sees trees, leaves not withering, fruit not failing and, in fact, bearing every month. Healing is being experienced. The river is bringing transformation almost everywhere it goes.

Evidently, even though the move of God, the move of the Spirit, initially comes to encourage and re-inspire us, we must not stop there. It is not about having great meetings and people getting drunk with the Spirit, though I love those things. In the long run we must venture out from the walls of the church and take the river to our community. Without that we make the same mistakes as previous moves of God, where we self-indulge in the river.

So, whenever a church experiences a move of God it is mission critical to then focus them toward the reason the Holy Spirit does this; to get their focus off themselves and onto the needs in their local, national and international communities. Such thinking must be continually reinforced at every level of church life.

Settling a Local Church into a Move of the Spirit

Eventually, the move of the Spirit will become a part of the DNA of the local church. As such, it then becomes necessary to bring some structure around what God is doing. It cannot just be a constant *free for all*.

I have found that it works well to designate certain meetings as dedicated to the move of the Spirit. Traditionally, I made Sunday nights that focus. Those who wanted to experience the move of the Spirit had a meeting they could go to, while those who weren't so comfortable with what was happening, well they could safely go to Sunday morning.

Extended meetings are brilliant, as explained previously, but soon the life of the church, in terms of teaching, discipling, training, caring and other essentials, needs to be reintroduced, so every week there is opportunity for the church to be exposed to the river of God, but church life continues.

No matter what is happening in a church, there is no substitute for good *church growth principles*. What a move of God should achieve is:

- To bring an increase in corporate love, worship and celebration of the life of Jesus amongst the congregation.

- A re-inspiring toward the mission of the church.

- To bring people to a place of deeper passion for Jesus.

- To bring back the passion for the call and gift of God on each other's lives; for an intense desire to once again serve with those callings and gifts.

- To bring an increased hunger for seeing people who don't know Jesus come to His saving grace.

In other words, not only should our personal and corporate love for Jesus demonstrate a huge increase, but so should the outward focus of the church. That's why when a move of God is happening, it is important to teach on such subjects as personal destiny, personal giftings, the call of God, the purpose of the church, and the invasion of the Kingdom of God into our communities. Without an outflow of the encounters people are having with the Holy Spirit, the local church will eventually implode on itself as people become frustrated with their personal empowerment, wanting to do something with it, yet not knowing how or what. At the very least, the power of the Spirit that people are experiencing must be focussed toward outreach, praying for people in their communities and leading people to Christ.

What About the People Who Never Seem to Get Touched or Receive from the Holy Spirit?

This is one of the most frequently asked questions when the Holy Spirit moves for a period of time in a church: "Why did everyone get touched but I felt nothing? Nothing ever happens to me." Earlier in this book I mentioned the man who said this to me and how I encouraged him to surrender and go with leaning to the left, and how the Holy Spirit then overpowered him. However, every church will have people that no matter how much they are prayed for, just never seem to receive anything.

Unfortunately, Christians who come from certain legalistic denominational backgrounds can seem, at times, to have an inbuilt resistance to things of the Spirit. It may be that they don't want this, but the infection and defilement, of what for some may have been years of involvement in such churches, has simply created a major blockage to anything to do with Holy Spirit freedom.

It's something that may not be in their heart or attitude, but certainly controls their inner being. I know this was the case with me and receiving the Baptism of the Holy Spirit. Initially, I was prayed for on two separate occasions to receive the Holy Spirit and couldn't. It became desperate and eventually I broke through and had a great encounter with the Holy Spirit.

On reflection of why it was so hard, I began to realise that I had, over a number of years, built into my heart a barrier to the Holy Spirit. I had spent a great deal of time opposing the understanding of the Baptism of the Holy Spirit and, in particular, the gift of speaking in tongues. This built a barrier that took prayer and desperation to break down. I thank God it eventually did and I was able to receive the Baptism of the Spirit. I don't understand this! But it's something I have observed all too frequently.

The first thing that needs to be spoken to a person who seems unable to receive is, "It is not your fault. It is not because you have sin in your life. It is not because God is not pleased with you. I have seen non-Christians receive the Holy Spirit and become drunk with the Spirit. I have witnessed many who I would have considered the most rebellious in my congregation easily receive the power of God, and the most saintly and righteous person receive nothing." The truth is, God is sovereign and He will touch whom He will touch and not touch whom He chooses not to touch. Why, it seems, He does this, I have no idea.

So what is the answer? Stay open in your heart, keep getting prayed for, keep going up on the altar calls, keep yourself hungry for the breakthrough. The reason is that I have seen, dozens and dozens of times, the most seemingly resistant and difficult person experience a breakthrough. If you stay open the breakthrough will come.

Secondly, even though everyone around you may be laughing and drunk in the Holy Spirit, that may not be what you need at that moment. Maybe you just need to cry and receive healing first! How the Holy Spirit chooses to touch one person versus another is His business. Our business is to stay open and receive.

Thirdly, I know for my life I have often received powerful things from the Holy Spirit without being slain in the Spirit, without getting drunk in the Spirit, without receiving the holy laughter.

The issue is never that a person should respond in a particular way in order to get touched with the Holy Spirit. The issue is to stay open and receive. Oftentimes the receiving is in quietness of spirit, in an atmosphere of personal peace and stillness, and that is just as powerful and significant as the person drunk in the Spirit.

What About the People Who are Put Off by the Manifestations of the Spirit?

There will always be some people who don't like the manifestations of the Holy Spirit and feel uncomfortable when it is happening. I understand this. My encouragement is that nobody is forced to participate. I give permission for people to opt out, and that is okay. What I do say, however, is don't be critical of what is happening to others. A critical spirit, if left unchecked, will eventually choke the life of the Spirit and you will become defiled.

The Move of God and Church Growth

I only want to touch on this briefly. No matter what is happening in a church it still needs to grow numerically. The aspects of what make a church a church must continue on, because people still have needs and require pastoral support. If a church does not experience growth it will often stagnate and turn in on itself.

When I was asked to run support for pastors who were experiencing the Toronto Blessing, I began monthly support meetings. These meetings were cross-denominational and continued on for over 12 years. In the first few years all I did was pray for people and talk about the move of the Spirit and the various dynamics revolving around it, but it became evident that more was needed. For instance, anyone who has experienced a move of the Spirit consistently over a long period of time will testify to the fact that a move of God does not always equate to a church growing. All too often it is quite the opposite. So even with the amazing things the Holy Spirit is doing, there still needs to be put in place the disciplines of church growth. Pastors need to become students of what makes a great church. Even a small church in a small community should never settle for the status quo, but always be looking to grow, improve and provide for the needs of their community.

It is with that in mind that I want to commend the reader to one of the most practical and empowering tools to assist with understanding what a healthy church should look like, and what needs to be done to bring growth to any church. It is called *Natural Church Development*. *The Natural Church Development Survey* discovered that there were eight essential qualities a healthy and growing church exhibited and, given that these eight characteristics were in a local church, it would naturally grow. Their site is easily found on the internet.

Pastoring a Congregation Through a Move of the Spirit

One of the most extraordinary aspects of any sustained move of the Spirit is the supernatural way the Holy Spirit flushes issues in people's lives to the surface. Whenever I have witnessed a move of the Spirit over extended periods, unresolved issues of the heart soon rise up. For instance, unresolved issues of sexual abuse and rape, personal hurts, interpersonal conflicts and unforgiveness, and the like. Heart issues have to be faced up to and biblically dealt with. Instead of allowing the normal structures of support to close down, they need to be reinforced to provide a platform for heart issues to be safely addressed. The small group structure is strategic to this process. It is important to realise that if a church does implement a series of extended meetings, even-tually the church will need to resort back to *normal life* in terms of its weekly meetings. Therefore, retaining this in some form, even during extended meetings, is important.

As previously stated, the Holy Spirit, when moving in power amongst the congregation, will also surface a new sense of destiny and calling. People will want to do something. Consequently they will need to be assisted to move into their ministries. There is a difference between teaching, which is the impartation of information, versus training, which is the shaping of a person to be effective in their life's mandate. Therefore the process of identifying, training and releasing people into their personal callings must be of highest priority for a church consistently moving in the power of the Spirit. I stress that this is not about teaching a Bible study, though it may be a part of it, rather, it's training and developing people and releasing them. In fact, this is the biblical mandate for the five-fold ministry:

And He gave some as apostles, and some as prophets, and some as evangelists, and some as pastors and teachers, for the equipping of the saints for the work of service, to the building up of the body of Christ... (Ephesians 4:11-12)

The effect is that the role of a pastor, for instance, is to train people to pastor, not to do the pastoring. It is a complete radicalisation of thinking that must be adopted. People think their pastor is there to pastor them. This is incredibly debilitating for the advancement of the Kingdom of God.

When someone needs visiting in hospital who should do that? Certainly not the pastor. The pastor trains and equips people to do hospital visitation. If someone requests the pastor to go to a home and pray for someone who is sick, the pastor's initial response must be "No". They train and equip people to do that, and then release them to go and do the praying. How are people going to allow an outflow of all that Holy Spirit influence and empowerment if this is not the directive from which the local church is operating? A major reconstruction of thinking must take place if the church is to gain the full impact of a move of God.

Fire Starters in the Congregation

One of the obvious things that soon becomes evident in a church experiencing a move of the Spirit is that some people just seem to get so easily touched by the Holy Spirit. The temptation is to become critical of them. Often you may hear it said, "Oh, there they go again, always the same ones behaving like that."

But such comments expose the fact that those being critical do not understand the workings of the Holy Spirit. In almost every congregation where I have experienced a move of God there will be people who simply are more open and receptive than others. It is best illustrated like an alcoholic. They are so *full of alcohol* that it just takes a small drink to get them going again. And so with the Holy Spirit, for some, it's just a small drink of the rivers of the Spirit and they are full again, and drunk in the Holy Spirit. In fact, the Lord will give to congregations such people for the express purpose of helping the flow of the Spirit to start quickly and easily. They are often called *fire starters*. They are the first ones to be prayed for, they quickly start experiencing the manifestations of the Spirit, and from them comes an overflow of the river of God on to others. And so the move of the Spirit quickly spreads throughout a congregation.

They should never be criticised nor rejected by a congregation; they should be nurtured and encouraged. It is understood that sometimes they can become excessive, but as with children experiencing for the first time a new toy or new environment, their excitement can get a little overwhelming and excessive. Gentle directing soon brings this into some semblance of order.

When the Holy Spirit Does Not Move in Power

Unfortunately there are places where no matter what you do, it seems the heavens are shut up. I used to feel bad about this; that somehow I was to blame for not bringing the expected move of the Spirit. However, I came to understand something so important:

For the one who sows to his own flesh will from the flesh reap corruption, but the one who sows to the Spirit will from the Spirit reap eternal life. (Galatians 6:8)

Eternal life is experienced now. I've met people who testify by their lives over this. Some people who are believers exude a life flow, the Holy Spirit just seems to ooze out of them. Some churches are like that. You walk into the atmosphere of the church and right from the beginning there is something there that is clearly Holy Spirit orientated.

And yet, some churches have great people, great leadership and pastors and maybe even great music. However, the atmosphere just seems devoid of energetic Holy Spirit atmosphere. I realised that in such an environment, where there has been little sowing in the Spirit, no matter what I did it was almost impossible to get a breakthrough. The fault was not mine, but the congregation's who had failed to engender a culture of openness and receptivity to the things of the Spirit. They may agree to the things of the Spirit, but a move of the Spirit is more than just agreement. There must be a culture of loving the things of the Spirit and encouragement for the Holy Spirit's movement. To the shame of many so-called Pentecostal churches, many people have not experienced the Baptism of the Holy Spirit. The church is Pentecostal by association only. The gifts of the Spirit may be agreed to and encouraged, but there is no genuine attempt to encourage the congregation to be movers in the gifts. The move of the Spirit has been relegated to theory and belief, but no action.

...holding to a form of godliness, although they have denied its power; Avoid such men as these. (2 Timothy 3:5)

I pray that we are not these people; talking about the power of God, living an apparent life of godliness, yet there is no clear manifestation of the power or the gifts of the Spirit flowing in their lives.

In such an environment it is extremely difficult to see the river of God freely flow. I pray, "God protect us from the religious bondage that would agree to the Holy Spirit's power and yet not actively pursue that same power!"

Understanding the Difference Between Revival, Renewal, Refreshing, Reformation and Revolution

There is much criticism concerning moves of the Spirit due to the confusion that comes by the incorrect use of terminology. For instance, a move of the Spirit can be occurring in a congregation and it begins to be referred to as a revival. And of course it is not a revival. The Toronto Blessing has become extensively criticised, I believe, because of this incorrect use of terminology.

Some simple definitions are as follows:

- Revival – taking something dead and reviving it and bringing transformation.

- Renewal – taking something not functioning with life and renewing it/bringing life to it.

- Refreshing – taking something tired and injecting new passion and life to it.

- Reformation – taking something out of shape and disfigured, and reforming it to proper structure and format.

- Revolution – complete transformation of society.

Revival is traditionally considered to be a move of God that sees the community outside the walls of the local church impacted and ultimately transformed. Personally I would prefer the description of this to be that of revolution; a community experiencing such impact of the Holy Spirit, a revolution is occurring. The structures, the prosperity, the crime rates, the schools and other aspects of the community are being transformed.

But generally what we see happening with moves of the Holy Spirit is renewal. I believe that is what the Toronto Blessing was. A local church is renewed. It began with a measure of life, but needed something of an injection of supernatural life to propel the congregation into new levels of passion and enthusiasm. When this is happening, church becomes exciting, the meetings transformational, and Christians are fired up for more of God and more enthusiastic for His purposes. But it should not stay there. Renewal and refreshing should create an advancement for the local church's missional activity and ultimately bring revival and revolution.

It has been my joy and privilege to see the Holy Spirit do just this in a small and troubled community in New Zealand. Kawerau is a small rural town in the North Island of New Zealand. Its main place of employment is a pulp and paper timber mill which, like many similar facilities, has reduced the number it employs. Consequently, Kawerau has one of the highest unemployment rates in New Zealand and one of the highest crime rates. Undergirding much of the economy is the unseen economy of drugs and alcohol.

In Kawerau is a small church, the Kawerau Community Church. The pastor, a close friend of mine, has always been a lover of the move of the Spirit. Pastoring a church with many young people from horrendous backgrounds has been a challenge but Pastors Matai and Cissie Bennett remained faithful to their entrustment. I have stood with him through the great times and the difficult times, and could always go there and very quickly start moving in the Holy Spirit and the power of God would move.

In June 2014 I was able to take a group of young people from America into this town and have a public meeting. The Lord moved in one of the largest Christian meetings in living memory. At the end of the meeting, over 100 young people came forward giving their lives to Jesus Christ. For a small community like Kawerau and a church like Pastor Matai's, this was a major move of God. The remarkable thing was that the next day 52 young people were seen praying in their school grounds for their school and teachers. On that same day, in the afternoon, a group of young people were in the main street of Kawerau praying for their town.

Eventually Pastor Matai and I agreed that something special was happening and so he commenced a series of meetings five nights a week. We coined the move a *love revival* amongst young people. The effect was dramatic, to say the least. Every night of the meetings, for several months, there were young people who had never given their lives to Christ coming forward for salvation. Eventually the impact was such that the police said the crime rate in the town had dropped.

The local school encouraged Pastor Matai to continue with the meetings due to the positive impact it was having in the community. Even the local gang was being impacted. The community was experiencing transformation.

After serving the Lord for over 30 years in New Zealand, moving around my nation seeking to bring moves of the Spirit, here was clear evidence that a church moving in the power of God could transition to seeing a community changed. In reality, what else would impact these young people in such a way as to transform their lives except a powerful encounter with the Holy Spirit? Many of these young people had experienced the most horrendous of experiences and so required something dramatic and powerful to arrest their attention and see their lives changed. The Holy Spirit has done that, and now money and opportunities for advancement are coming into Kawerau through Pastor Matai to further the transformational work of the Holy Spirit.

I was asked many years ago to speak to a large group of Pentecostal pastors on how it was that I was able to retain such a passion and *fire* for the ministry. My answer was simple: "I am constantly in a move of God, of the Holy Spirit. That keeps me fired up!" And now, at the time of this writing, I am assisting in the first genuine revival I have personally witnessed in New Zealand.

I say, "Let the Holy Spirit move!"